JAVASERVER PAGES

in eas

MIKE MCGRATH

COMPUTER
STEP

In easy steps is an imprint of Computer Step
Southfield Road . Southam
Warwickshire CV47 OFB . England

http://www.ineasysteps.com

Notice of Liability

Every effort has been made to ensure that this book contains accurate and current information. However, Computer Step and the author shall not be liable for any loss or damage suffered by readers as a result of any information contained herein.

Trademarks

All trademarks are acknowledged as belonging to their respective companies.

Printed and bound in the United Kingdom

ISBN 1-84078-197-1

Contents

13 Connecting JSP to MySQL   159

14 A JSP online shop   169

Index   187

Introducing JavaServer Pages

Welcome to the exciting world of JavaServer Pages (JSP). This chapter introduces JSP with an explanation of what it is, how it works and what it can achieve. Instructions describe how to download and install the free Java class libraries and the free Tomcat server to establish a development environment for JSP on your own computer. A first simple example then demonstrates JSP in action within this environment.

Covers

Chapter One

JSP in this book

This book is an introduction to JavaServer Pages server-side technology, giving examples to demonstrate each step.

JSP allows developers to easily create and maintain information-rich dynamic Web pages.

Currently most Web pages are delivered by the Apache Web server running on a UNIX or Linux operating platform, while the most popular PC operating system is Microsoft Windows. This book conveniently instructs you how to establish a local server/client environment under Windows where JSP content can be developed. This content may then be uploaded to a JSP-enabled Web server, running on any platform, for active service on the Internet.

The examples given throughout this book detail the source code and the resultant output that appears in a Web browser.

What you need to know

JSP harnesses the power of the Java programming language in HTML pages, so it is expected that you are familiar with HTML. The reader with some knowledge of Java will find it easier to understand the more advanced possibilities of JSP.

This book includes a chapter that provides the reader with a basic knowledge of Java to help those new to Java to grasp the examples.

You do not need to be a Java guru to use JavaServer Pages.

Required software

The Java Software Development Kit (SDK) needs to be installed on your PC to make the Java class libraries and compiler available to the JSP environment. A JSP Web server also needs to be installed so that JSP examples can be tried locally.

This chapter instructs you how to download and install the free Java SDK and the free Tomcat Web server to establish a JSP development environment on your own computer.

What is JavaServer Pages?

JavaServer Pages is a technology that allows Web pages to be created dynamically from the Web server so that the page content can be varied according to circumstances.

This can be used, for instance, to provide custom pages according to the identity of the user, the type of Web browser they are using, information they have provided or selections they have made.

JSP documents are written in plain text and have a **.jsp** file extension. They use tags, like those in HTML or XML, to denote JSP elements.

A JSP element is used to dynamically insert content into a page. It can be used for many purposes, such as getting information from a database or retrieving user preferences.

JSP elements can contain scriptlets, written in the Java programming language, to provide the logic to determine which content should be generated for a Web page.

Alternatively the logic can reside in a server-based resource, such as a JavaBean component, that can be accessed by a JSP tag to generate the content of a page.

The separation of logic from other content is a particularly appealing feature of JSP as it makes page maintenance simpler.

Like the Java servlet technology from which it is derived, JavaServer Pages is completely platform-independent so requires no modifications to run on any platform. It shares the 'Write Once, Run Anywhere' philosophy that is common to all Java technologies.

The JSP specification has been developed by Sun Microsystems in collaboration with leading software suppliers. Sun has made it freely available with the stated goal of having every Web server and application server support the JSP interface.

JavaServer Pages is an important part of Sun's Java 2 Enterprise Edition platform that provides a highly scalable architecture for enterprise applications.

How does JSP work?

A typical JSP page will contain a number of JSP elements along with HTML markup elements and other textual content.

A JSP page is always compiled before it is processed by the server.

The first time that the JSP page is called by a Web browser the JSP-enabled Web server compiles the page into executable code. The compiled code is then processed by the server which executes the JSP logic elements and delivers the results to the browser.

It is important to note that the compiled version of the JSP page is stored on the server for subsequent calls to that page. This avoids the need to compile the original page code each time the browser loads the JSP page and speeds up the process considerably.

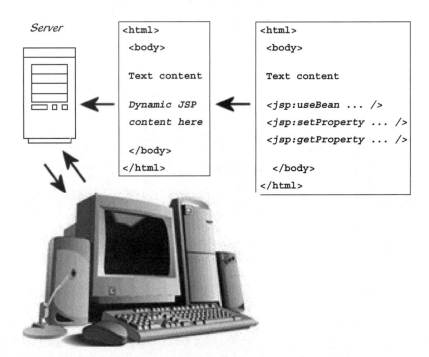

The process of loading a JSP page, from a JSP-enabled server into a PC's Web browser, is illustrated above.

When the server receives the browser request, the JSP processor generates the page to include both the static HTML and text content together with the dynamic JSP content. The total content of the generated page is finally delivered to the PC for display in the browser window.

Advantages of JavaServer Pages

JSP is not the only way to add extra functionality to a server but it does offer significant advantages over other methods such as the popular Common Gateway Interface (CGI):

Platform independence

JSP is an extension of the Java servlet technology that is supported by all major Web servers and application servers. Java servlets use the 'Write Once, Run Anywhere' principal which does not restrict their usefulness to a specific operating system.

Efficient processing

For more on the Common Gateway Interface and the Perl scripting language refer to 'CGI & Perl in easy steps':

A servlet runs on the server in a continuous process that creates a separate thread for each request it receives. This is more efficient than the CGI method that creates a new process for each request. It also means that a servlet has access to continuous resources, such as database connections and client state, that are loaded in the process memory. These remain available until the servlet application is closed and the process is, therefore, terminated.

Solid performance

The Java programming language places greater emphasis on error handling than other programming languages such as C or C++. Many of the errors which are caught when the JSP pages are compiled into executable code, by the Java compiler during development, would only surface at runtime with a scripting language like Perl. This ensures that JSP will function correctly.

Improved security

Servlets do not communicate with the server in the same direct manner as CGI scripts but, instead, use special interfaces which are not vulnerable to security attacks.

Highly scalable

The portability of JSP servlets means that they can be developed and tested on a PC running a Windows operating system using the Java SDK and a JSP-enabled server, like Tomcat. They can take full advantage of the rich features of all the Java technologies, such as Java Database Connectivity (JDBC) for database access. Once satisfied with the servlet application, it may be then deployed on a much more powerful server that might typically be running Apache Web server software on the Linux operating system.

Installing the Java SDK

The Java Software Development Kit (SDK) should be installed on your computer before you can create JavaServer Pages locally. This contains the Java code compiler that is used by the JSP processor.

The Java SDK is freely available for download from Sun Microsystems' website at `http://java.sun.com`. The standard edition is suitable for computers running on Microsoft Windows 95, 98, Me, NT, 2000 and XP.

Separate versions of the Java SDK are also available for Linux or Solaris operating systems.

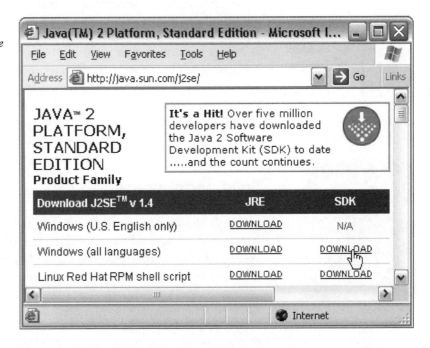

Comprehensive documentation for the Java SDK is also available as a separate download from the Sun website.

The download comprises a single executable file that will begin installation of the Java SDK when it is run. During the installation, when prompted, either accept the default installation path or enter a preferred location where the Java files are to be installed. For instance, **C:\Java** is a convenient choice.

After choosing a location for the Java SDK, the installer's **Select Components** dialog box will offer a choice of components to be installed. It is only essential to install the Program Files so you should check that option and ensure that all others are unchecked. Following component selection, all the necessary Java class libraries and tools will be installed at the chosen location.

SDK setup and test

The tools to compile and run Java programs are normally operated from a command prompt that typically appears as **C:\>**.

These tools are located in the **bin** folder of the Java installation directory and can be made available from anywhere on the computer by adding their location to the system path.

In modern versions of Windows, like XP, click on Start > Settings > Control Panel > System > Advanced > Environment Variables, then select the **Path** variable and click the **Edit** button. Add the location of the **bin** folder to the end of the path line like below:

If there is a CLASSPATH environment variable on your system it should be deleted, or at least amended to include the current directory. For instance, Windows 9x users could adjust their autoexec.bat with a SET CLASSPATH=.; statement.

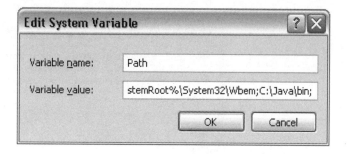

On computers running on a Windows 9x operating system the Java **bin** folder can be added to the system path by editing a line in the **autoexec.bat** file. Open up **autoexec.bat** in a text editor and add the location at the end of the path line so that it looks like this:

```
SET PATH=C:\WINDOWS;C:\WINDOWS\COMMAND;C:\JAVA\BIN;
```

Now, re-boot your computer to apply the new path settings.

To test that the Java tools are now available on the system path, type **javac** at a command prompt and the Java compiler should present a list of options if the installation is correct.

If the system cannot find the Java compiler adjust the path settings to exactly match those shown above then re-boot and retry the test.

When Java responds to the **javac** command correctly the system is ready to start compiling and running Java code.

Installing the Tomcat server

In order to develop JSP pages on your own computer there must be a JSP-enabled server installed. The standard reference server for JSP is the Tomcat server which is part of the Jakarta project.

Visit the Jakarta project at `http://jakarta.apache.org/ binindex.html` to discover a series of possible Tomcat downloads as Release, Milestone or Nightly builds. To get the latest stable version for use on a Windows platform you should download the Release version, in binary format, by following the download links on the Web page.

The links will lead you to a list of download files similar to those in the illustration below:

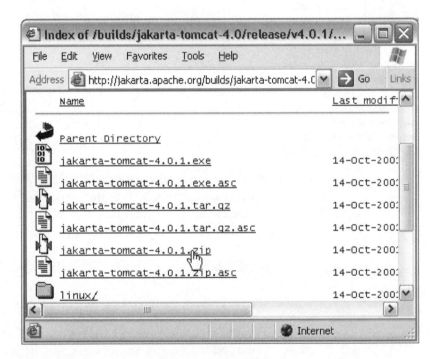

For Windows, download the zip file then unzip its entire contents to a new appropriately named directory location, such as **C:\Tomcat**. This creates a directory structure under a directory named **jakarta-tomcat-4.0.1** (or similar for other versions). Its **doc** sub-directory contains a **readme** file giving important information about installing and running the Tomcat server.

Tomcat uses an environment variable named **JAVA_HOME** to indicate the location of the Java SDK top-level directory, such as **C:\Java**, and another variable named **CATALINA_HOME** to indicate the location of Tomcat's jakarta-level directory, such as **C:\Tomcat\jakarta-tomcat-4.0.1.**

In Windows XP click on Start > Settings > Control Panel > System > Advanced > Environment Variables, then click on the **New** button and add these new variables and their values.

The Tomcat installation procedure may vary – be sure to check the installation instructions for the version you download.

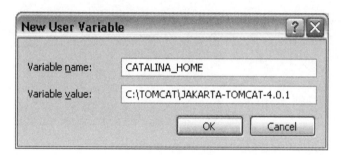

On Windows 9x systems open the **autoexec.bat** file and set these environment variables by adding the lines shown below:

```
SET JAVA_HOME=C:\JAVA
SET CATALINA_HOME=C:\TOMCAT\JAKARTA-TOMCAT-4.0.1
```

Save the modifications then re-boot the system to apply the new environment variable settings. These can then be tested from a command prompt by typing **ECHO**, followed by a space, then the name of the variable enclosed inside a pair of **%** characters. This will return the value that the variable represents on your computer.

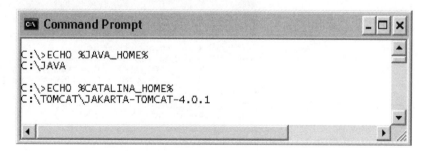

Running & testing Tomcat

The Tomcat server is a no-frills application that is launched by running a batch file named **startup.bat** which is located in Tomcat's **bin** directory. The absolute address of this file will be something like **C:\Tomcat\jakarta-tomcat-4.0.1\bin\startup.bat**.

The startup and shutdown batch files can also run from a command line.

Navigate to this **bin** directory and double-click on the **startup.bat** icon to attempt to launch Tomcat. If the attempt succeeds, a command prompt window opens which announces that the Tomcat server is running, and looks like the window below:

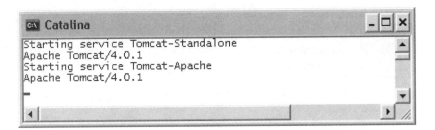

This window is where the server process is running so it must be left open as long as the Tomcat service is required to be available.

The server should not be stopped by simply closing this window but should, instead, be shut down properly by running the **shutdown.bat** file in Tomcat's **bin** directory. Navigate to the **bin** directory, then double-click on the **shutdown.bat** icon to stop Tomcat. This will close the server process window shown above.

It is common on Windows 9x operating systems for attempts to launch and stop Tomcat to be met with an error message, like the one shown below, protesting about a lack of environment space.

The solution is to increase the size of the memory space that is allocated for environment variables on your computer.

Right-click on the **startup.bat** icon in the **bin** directory, select **Properties** from the context menu, then click the **Memory** tab. Now change the **initial environment** value from **auto** to **4096** and click **apply** to set the environment space to 4Kb (4096 bytes). Repeat this procedure for **shutdown.bat** then double-click on the **startup.bat** icon to launch the Tomcat server.

The port can be changed to the standard port 80 by editing Tomcat's conf/ server.xml file. This book retains port 8080 for Tomcat to avoid conflicts with other Web servers that may be running.

With Tomcat running, the server can be tested by calling up a page via Tomcat from a Web browser on the same computer. By default the Tomcat service is configured to listen for HTTP requests on port 8080, so you can call up its default home page by entering the URL http://localhost:8080 into the browser address field. When Tomcat is installed correctly a page similar to the one shown below will appear in the browser window.

Make desktop shortcuts to the startup and shutdown batch files so Tomcat can be conveniently started and stopped.

Hello World

With the Tomcat service running correctly, a first JSP page can be created to display the traditional 'Hello World' message when viewed in a Web browser, via the Tomcat server.

JSP source files are plain text documents that can be created in any simple text editor, such as Windows Notepad. They are just like HTML documents but have additional JSP elements. Anything in a JSP document that is not part of a JSP element is called **template text**. In the example code below the three JSP elements are shown in bold type, whereas the template text is shown in normal type.

hello.jsp

In Java, text strings must be enclosed in quotes and statements must be terminated with a semi-colon.

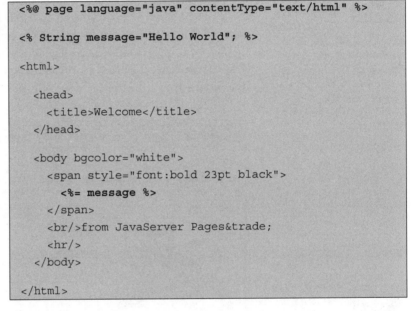

```
<%@ page language="java" contentType="text/html" %>

<% String message="Hello World"; %>

<html>

  <head>
    <title>Welcome</title>
  </head>

  <body bgcolor="white">
    <span style="font:bold 23pt black">
      <%= message %>
    </span>
    <br/>from JavaServer Pages&trade;
    <hr/>
  </body>

</html>
```

Detailed explanation of the different JSP elements are given in the next chapter of this book.

The first JSP element in the code above is the standard first line of a JSP document that describes to the JSP processor the document's MIME type and the scripting language used in the JSP elements.

The second JSP element in this example declares a Java String-type variable that can be used to store strings of text characters. In this case, the variable is given the name of **message**, and is assigned a text string value of 'Hello World'.

The third JSP element in the example above will insert the value of the **message** variable as text content in the final generated page.

The example code is saved as a file named **hello.jsp** and is placed in Tomcat's **ROOT** directory where the server expects to find any pages that are requested from it by a Web browser. The absolute address of this directory will be something like **C:\Tomcat\jakarta-tomcat-4.0.1\webapps\ROOT**.

To call this first page from a Web browser just enter the URL `http://localhost:8080/hello.jsp` into the browser's address field and the output shown below should be displayed.

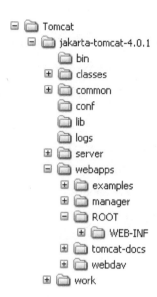

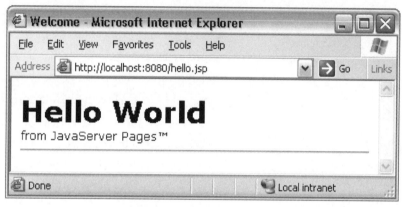

Click on **View** then **Source** on the browser menu to reveal the source code of the generated HTML page. Notice that the JSP elements no longer appear and the value of the **message** text string has been inserted into the page's body.

*Java is a case-sensitive language so you must ensure that code is capitalised correctly. For instance, the Java **String** keyword will not be recognised if it is written as **STRING** or **string**.*

Analysing the JSP process

The steps involved in processing the Hello World example on the previous page can be examined more closely in order to gain a better understanding of the JSP process.

hello.jsp

1 When the Tomcat server receives a HTTP request for the **hello.jsp** page it first looks at its **ROOT** directory to see if the file exists. If the **hello.jsp** file is not found there the server will report an error, otherwise the process moves on to the next step.

hello$jsp.class

2 The JSP process then checks to see if a compiled executable version already exists for the requested page. With Tomcat, these are placed in a working directory that is named simply with an underscore character. The address of this directory will be something like **C:\Tomcat\jakarta-tomcat-4.0.1\work\localhost_**. The compiled version of the **hello.jsp** page is a Java class file called **hello$jsp.class**. If this class file is found in the working directory, the JSP process will execute the code and deliver the page to the Web browser, otherwise it moves on again to the next step.

hello$jsp.java

3 On the first occasion that **hello.jsp** is requested, the server will not find a compiled version of the page so it must create one. To do this it first builds a Java source code file that integrates the template text and the JSP elements which are contained in **hello.jsp**. The resulting human-readable file is named **hello$jsp.java** and is placed in Tomcat's working directory at **work\localhost_**.

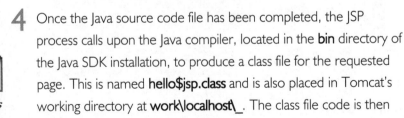

hello$jsp.class

4 Once the Java source code file has been completed, the JSP process calls upon the Java compiler, located in the **bin** directory of the Java SDK installation, to produce a class file for the requested page. This is named **hello$jsp.class** and is also placed in Tomcat's working directory at **work\localhost_**. The class file code is then executed and the page is delivered to the browser.

Basic elements

This chapter introduces the six basic JSP elements. These comprise three directive elements, which allow you to supply information to the JSP processor, and three scripting elements, which enable you to embed functional Java code in the page. Examples also show how to add descriptive comments and how to escape characters from recognition by the JSP processor.

Covers

Chapter Two

Page directive element

Directive elements are used to provide information about the constant page specifications to the JSP processor. The tag of all directive elements begins with **<%@** and end with **%>**.

The directive element tag first specifies the directive type name, then pre-defined attributes to which the information is assigned. So the general syntax for directive elements looks like this:

```
<%@ directiveType attrib1="value1" attrib2="value2" %>
```

Attribute values must always be enclosed in quotes.

The most common directive element is the **page** directive that appears at the top of each JSP page of code to define the scripting language used in that page. Usually, Java will be specified by the **language** attribute but this could, in fact, be another recognised scripting language, such as VBScript or JavaScript.

Additionally the **page** directive specifies the MIME type to be used for the page to be generated by JSP in a **contentType** attribute. For a HTML page the assigned value will be **text/html**.

A typical **page** directive containing this information will appear as:

```
<%@ page language="java" contentType="text/html" %>
```

The **contentType** attribute may additionally specify a character set for a page to be generated by the JSP page for foreign language pages. This information is added to a **charset** sub–attribute after the MIME type. For instance, a page to be generated using a Japanese language character set could be specified like this:

```
<%@ page contentType="text/html;charset=Shift_JIS" %>
```

For more details on error handling please see Chapter 7.

The **page** directive may also, optionally, specify the URL of a page to which the browser should be redirected in the event of an error occurring in the code on the page. This can be assigned to an **errorPage** attribute in the page directive element.

If the page is itself to be used as an error page then the **page** directive should contain an **isErrorPage** attribute set to **true** which makes an implicit **exception** variable available to examine and handle any page errors.

The **page** directive element has further optional attributes called **autoFlush**, **buffer** and **session** whose default values allow session tracking and automatic flushing of an 8kb page buffer. The **autoFlush**, **buffer** and **session** default values are normally satisfactory, so these attributes can usually be omitted.

A full list of all common **page** directive attributes, together with a description and their default value, is given in the table below:

*Just like Java, JSP is case–sensitive so care must be taken to ensure the correct capitalisation of code. For instance, the **page** keyword will not be recognised if it is written as Page or PAGE.*

Attribute Name	Default Value	Description
autoFlush	true	Automatically flushes the page buffer when it becomes full
buffer	8kb	Sets the buffer size for the page
contentType	text/html	Specifies the MIME type to be used for a page to be generated from the JSP page
errorPage	none	States a URL to where the user is redirected if an error occurs
import	none	Makes available methods within the specified Java class
info	none	Optional text to describe the page at administrator level
isErrorPage	false	Gives access to a JSP implicit **exception** variable when true to allow an error to be examined and handled
language	java	Defines the scripting language that is used on that page
session	true	Gives access to a JSP implicit **session** variable when true to allow the page to participate in an interactive user session

For more about sessions refer to Chapter 8 on Data Control.

Include directive element

The JSP **include** directive element is useful to merge the content of an external static file with the contents of a JSP page. The URI of the external file is assigned to a **file** attribute in the include directive tag and the contents of that file will be merged into the JSP page at the point where the element is placed.

*A JSP page may contain multiple **include** directive elements.*

The example below merges the JSP page with a simple text file that is placed in Tomcat's ROOT directory alongside the JSP page. Notice that the output inserts the contents of the included text file into the template text at the precise point where the **include** directive element appears in the JSP page.

include.txt

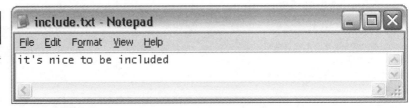

```
it's nice to be included
```

include.jsp

```
<%@ page language="java" contentType="text/html" %>

<html>
 <head> <title>Include Directive Demo</title> </head>
 <body bgcolor="white">
    Hello...
    <%@ include file="include.txt" %>
    ...it makes me feel good.
 </body>
</html>
```

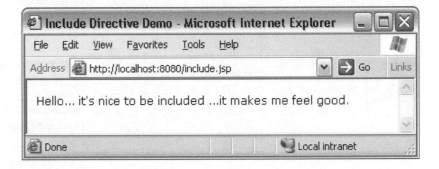

Hello... it's nice to be included ...it makes me feel good.

Taglib directive element

The JSP **taglib** directive element is used to specify the location of a library file containing custom JSP tag actions. This file will often be a compressed archive file with a **.jar** file extension.

The **taglib** directive tag must contain a **uri** attribute to specify the location of the library file. Also, it must contain a **prefix** attribute to specify a short name that can be used later to reference the library of custom tags.

In the following example the **taglib** directive gives the location of a custom tag library called **bartag.jar** and specifies a prefix of **bar** by which it may be referenced. This prefix is used in the next tag to set attribute values for a **Vbar** custom action tag that subsequently displays the assigned values as a bar chart.

taglib.jsp

```
<html>
 <head> <title>Taglib Directive Demo</title> </head>
 <body>
  <b><u>Monthly Sales</u></b><br/>
  <%@ taglib uri="WEB-INF/lib/bartag.jar" prefix="bar"%>
  <bar:Vbar width="200" height="75"
            bgcolor="#C0C0C0" fgcolor="#000000"
            values="4,3,6,8,7"  labels="J,F,M,A,M" />
 </body>
</html>
```

This custom tag library is one of many that are freely available on the Web – detailed advice on using tag libraries is given in Chapter 11.

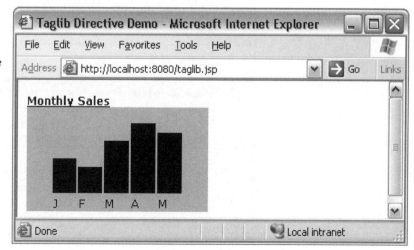

Scriptlet scripting element

Scriptlet elements allow small pieces of code to be added to a JSP page to provide logical functionality. The scriptlet tags begin with **<%** and end with **%>** and they may contain code written in the scripting language defined in the **page** directive for that page.

Scriptlet elements can be interspersed with template text but the code they contain must form valid scripting statements. Notice in the JSP page below that each scripting statement ends with a semi–colon as required by the Java language. This example displays the date at the time that the page is processed, then examines the date number (20 in this case). The scripting elements then write out a text string appropriate to whether the date number is odd or even.

scriptlet.jsp

The Java language is covered in more detail in Chapter 4.

```
<html>
 <head>
  <title>Scriptlet Scripting Element Demo</title>
 </head>
 <body>
 <% java.util.Date now = new java.util.Date(); %>

 Welcome to this page! <br/>
 It's now <% out.print(now);  %>  <br/>

 Today is an
 <% if(now.getDate() % 2 ==0)
        out.print("even number");
    else out.print("odd number"); %> day.
 </body>
</html>
```

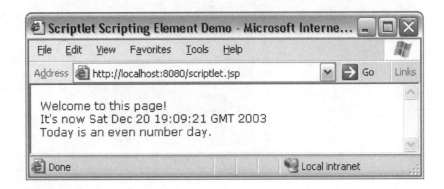

Expression scripting element

Expression elements are used to evaluate a single code expression then add the result to the JSP page output as a text string. The expression tags begin with **<%=** and end with **%>** and they may contain code written in the scripting language defined in the **page** directive for that page.

Expression elements can be freely mixed with template text but the code they contain must form a valid scripting expression. The expression should not, however, be terminated with a semi-colon as only a single expression is allowed in these elements.

The JSP page shown below uses two expression elements to produce the same sort of output as the example on the opposite page. A scripting element initially assigns the current date and time to a variable which is subsequently displayed by the first expression element. A second expression element examines the date number and writes out an appropriate text string.

expression.jsp

Adding a terminating semi-colon inside an expression element will cause an error.

```
<html>
 <head> <title>Expression Scripting Element Demo</title>
 </head>
 <body>
 <% java.util.Date now = new java.util.Date(); %>

 Welcome to this page! <br/>
 It's now <%= now %>  <br/>
 Today is an <%= (now.getDate() % 2 ==0) ?
                     "even number" : "odd number" %> day.
 </body>
</html>
```

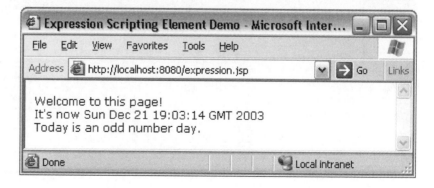

Declaration scripting element

The declaration scripting element begins with **<%!** and ends with **%>** and is used to declare variables or methods in the scripting language used in that JSP page.

Those same declarations could, of course, be made in plain scriptlet elements but the results have one very important difference – declarations made in scriptlet elements are available locally to all other code on that page, but declarations made within declaration elements are also available globally to other parallel requests for that page.

Declarations are initialised when the JSP page is first requested and are made available to scriptlets, and expressions throughout the page. Once initialised, they are also available to subsequent requests for that page. This can cause problems when multiple requests are made simultaneously so it is better to avoid declaration elements unless global availability is an absolute necessity.

The JSP page below creates a global counter that is first initialised at zero then incremented upon each request for that page:

declaration.jsp

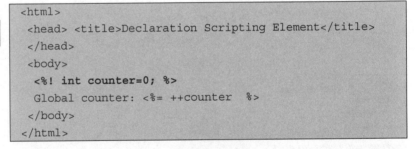

```html
<html>
 <head> <title>Declaration Scripting Element</title>
 </head>
 <body>
  <%! int counter=0; %>
  Global counter: <%= ++counter  %>
 </body>
</html>
```

Open this page in two browser windows then hit Refresh in either window to increment the counter. Change the declaration to a scriptlet element to see what difference this makes.

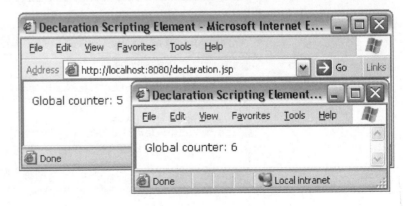

Adding comments

It is always a good idea to add comments to code to make it more comprehensible to third parties, or to yourself when revisiting the code after some time. Comments on a JSP page added between elements that begin **<%--** and end with **--%>** are ignored by the JSP processor. The example below includes both a JSP comment and a HTML comment.

```html
<html>
  <head> <title>Comment Elements</title> </head>
  <body>
   <%-- write a commented headline --%>
   <!-- today's front page headline -->
   <span style="font:bold 28pt">GOTCHA!</span>
   <br/>Another triumph for tabloid journalism
  </body>
</html>
```

comments.jsp

View the source code of the generated page to confirm that the JSP comment has been removed but the one for the HTML code is intact.

Escaping characters

Double quotes have a special meaning to the JSP processor because they are used as containers for attribute values. However, sometimes you will want to use double quote characters literally, perhaps to contain a quotation within a String attribute value, without the JSP processor attaching any special significance to it.

To include a backslash literally it must be preceded by a second escaping backslash.

The solution is to escape the character from recognition by preceding it with a \ backslash. This tells the JSP processor to treat the next character literally. Alternatively, single quotes could be used, nested inside double quotes.

A double quote can also be included using its special entity shorthand of **"** without attracting the attention of the JSP processor. Similarly an ampersand can be added with **&**.

The simple JSP page shown below demonstrates how each of these means of escaping characters from the processor appears in action:

escaping.jsp

```
<html>
  <head> <title>Escaping characters</title> </head>
  <body>
  <%= "Here are some 'nested quotes' " %> <br/>
  <%= "And here are \"escaped double quotes\" " %> <br/>
  <%= "And this is a \\ backslash character" %> <br/>
  <%= "Also you can use a double quote entity &quot; " %>
  <br/> <%= "Or an ampersand entity &amp; " %>
  </body>
</html>
```

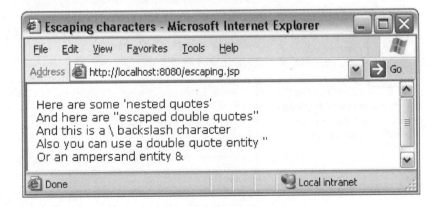

Action elements

JavaServer Pages defines a number of standard elements which can be used to perform actions when a JSP page is requested by a browser. This chapter explores each of these action elements and gives examples showing how they may be used.

Covers

Chapter Three

The useBean element

A JavaBean is simply a small Java program, written to comply with certain rules, that has been compiled into a Java class file. This can be placed in a folder within Tomcat's **classes** directory to make it available to the JSP processor.

The JSP **useBean** action element makes a JavaBean program accessible for scripting in a JSP page. This element, like all JSP action elements, has XML syntax that looks like this:

```
<jsp:useBean id="refName" class="folder.className" />
```

The **id** attribute is mandatory and assigns a name of your choice which can then be used to reference the bean's methods and properties in scripting in the JSP page.

A **class** attribute is added to the useBean element to specify the location and name of the particular JavaBean to be used. For instance, to use a JavaBean called **bean1.class** located in a folder called **mybeans**, within Tomcat's **classes** directory, the useBean **class** attribute would need to be assigned "mybeans.bean1".

Optionally a **scope** attribute can also be added in the useBean element to specify when the bean should be available with permissible values of **page**, **request**, **session** or **application. The** default, unless specified otherwise, is **page** – meaning that the bean methods and properties will be available during the life of the page.

In order to use features of the JavaBean it is essential to know the names of its methods and properties. The example on the opposite page uses a bean called **bean1** that has a String variable called **name** and three methods called **setName()**, **getName()** and **addStyle()**. The **id** sets a reference name of **myBean** for this JavaBean so that its methods can be used in scripting on that JSP page by appending their name with dot syntax, such as **myBean.setName()**.

The **setName()** method takes a single String argument, contained in double quotes inside its parentheses, that is assigned to the **name** variable in **bean1**. The value of this variable can be simply retrieved with the **getName()** method whereas the **addStyle()** method again gets the variable value but adds styling to the way it is displayed. Notice how the bean is reused with a different specified value.

useBean1.jsp

```html
<html>
 <head><title>useBean Demo</title></head>
 <body>

  <%-- Locate the bean and refer to it as myBean --%>
  <jsp:useBean id="myBean" class="mybeans.bean1"/>

  <%-- Set the name property using setName() --%>
  <% myBean.setName("JavaServer Pages&trade;");%>

  <%-- Reveal the name property using getName() --%>
  Name: <%= myBean.getName() %><br/>

  <%-- Reveal the stylized name using addStyle() --%>
  Stylized Name: <%= myBean.addStyle() %>

  <%-- Reset the name and show plain and stylized --%>
  <% myBean.setName("This JSP stuff is fun !"); %>
  Name: <%= myBean.getName() %><br/>
  Stylized Name: <%= myBean.addStyle() %>

 </body>
</html>
```

JavaBeans are demonstrated in more detail in Chapter 10.

*During JSP development Tomcat can be forced to reload changed classes by editing the **server.xml** file in Tomcat's **conf** folder – in the section headed **Define properties for each web application** add the line **<DefaultContext reloadable="true" />**.*

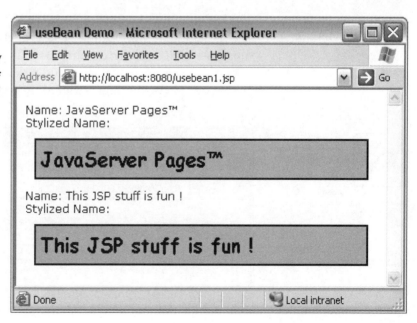

setProperty & getProperty elements

The JSP action elements **setProperty** and **getProperty** are used to specify and retrieve values from a JavaBean and are great for the non-programmer because they avoid contact with any Java code.

To utilise these action elements simply requires that you know the name and type of the JavaBean's properties. A value can then be assigned to a property using a **setProperty** element with this syntax:

```
<jsp:setProperty
   name="refName" property="propName" value="value" />
```

Third-party JavaBeans are supplied with instructions giving details of their properties, data types and methods.

Attempting to set a property with an inappropriate data type may cause an error. For instance, an integer type property will be expecting to be assigned an integer value, not a String value.

The **value** attribute can be replaced by a **param** attribute to specify a property value from a request parameter – more on this later.

Property values can be retrieved from the JavaBean with the **getProperty** action element, which has this syntax:

```
<jsp:getProperty name="refName" property="propName" />
```

The JSP page listed on the opposite page generates the output shown below. In this example, a **setProperty** action element supplies an initial property value to the bean. The Java code in the bean uses this value to calculate and assign values for its other properties. These are then retrieved by **getProperty** elements.

The source code for the bean2 JavaBean is listed fully on page 130.

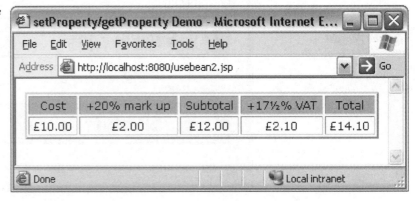

Cost	+20% mark up	Subtotal	+17½% VAT	Total
£10.00	£2.00	£12.00	£2.10	£14.10

useBean2.jsp

Notice that the cost property is set as a numeric value – the costPrice property that is retrieved is a formatted String version of the original cost property.

The full source code for the JavaBean used by this example is listed on *page 131.*

```html
<html>
<head>
<title>setProperty/getProperty Demo</title>
</head>
<body>
<%-- Find and instantiate the bean, myBean --%>
<jsp:useBean id="myBean" class="mybeans.bean2"/>

<%-- Specify an initial cost value --%>
<jsp:setProperty name="myBean"
                            property="cost" value="10.00" />

<table width="100%" border="2" cellpadding="2"
                            style="text-align:center">
<tr style="background:silver">
<td>Cost</td>
<td>+20% mark up</td>
<td>Subtotal</td>
<td>+17½% VAT</td>
<td>Total</td>
</tr>
<tr>
<td>
 <jsp:getProperty  name="myBean" property="costPrice" />
</td>
<td>
 <jsp:getProperty  name="myBean" property="markup" />
</td>
<td>
 <jsp:getProperty  name="myBean" property="subtotal" />
</td>
<td>
 <jsp:getProperty  name="myBean" property="vat" />
</td>
<td>
 <jsp:getProperty  name="myBean" property="total" />
</td>
</tr>
</table>
</body>
</html>
```

The include element

JSP provides an **include** action element in addition to the JSP **include** directive that was introduced in the previous chapter. Both allow the inclusion of content from other pages but are executed in subtly different ways.

Strictly speaking, the **include** *directive includes the actual content of the included page – whereas the* **include** *action element includes the response from the included page.*

The **include** directive is implemented at the time when the page is translated into a JSP servlet, so is ideal to incorporate static content that never changes. The **include** action element, on the other hand, is implemented at runtime when the JSP page is requested by a browser. This element is ideal to incorporate dynamic content that may change according to runtime conditions. For instance, the **include** element might incorporate different content according to the URL of the page calling an external JSP page.

The location of a page to be included is assigned to a **page** attribute in an **include** element tag, as demonstrated in this example:

page1.jsp
page2.jsp
page3.jsp

```
<%@ page language="java" contentType="text/html" %>
 <html>
  <head><title>Include Action Demo</title></head>
  <body bgcolor="white">

   <jsp:include page="nav.jsp" />

   <div style="background:silver; text-align:center;">
   This is Page [1 or 2 or 3] </div>
   </body>
 </html>
```

nav.jsp

```
<%@ page language="java" contentType="text/html" %>
<% String uri=request.getServletPath(); %>

<% if(uri.equals("/page1.jsp")) { %>
<a href="page2.jsp">Next Page &gt;&gt;</a> <br/>

<% } else if(uri.equals("/page2.jsp")) { %>
<a href="page1.jsp"> &lt;&lt; Previous Page</a> |
<a href="page3.jsp">Next Page &gt;&gt;</a> <br/>

<% } else if(uri.equals("/page3.jsp")) { %>
<a href="page2.jsp">&lt;&lt; Previous Page</a> <br/>
<% } %>
```

The included content is inserted at the point where the **include** *element appears then the remainder of the page is processed.*

In this example **page1.jsp**, **page2.jsp** and **page3.jsp** are identical, save for their page number, and each includes the **nav.jsp** page from their **include** action element. This included page identifies the page that has called it, using a Java function, then supplies HTML code to create navigation links appropriate to that page.

The user can now follow the links to navigate through each of these three pages, as shown in the illustrations below:

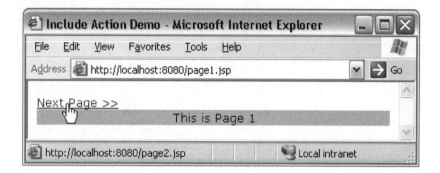

The scripting in **nav.jsp** *is explained in more detail later – for now, just note that the URI is returned from the function with a leading forward slash.*

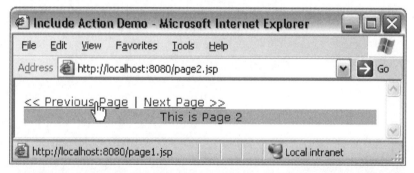

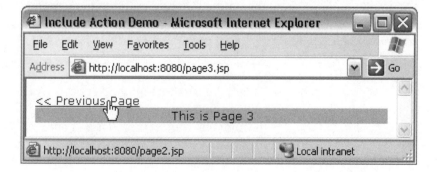

The forward element

The JSP **forward** action element is used to pass control from the current page to another JSP page. When it appears in a JSP page the control is immediately passed to the new page and processing of the original page ceases at once.

A **page** attribute is required in the **forward** action tag to specify the location of the page to which control will pass.

Typically a JSP page featuring **forward** elements will simply redirect control to an appropriate page, after performing some sort of conditional test, without producing any visible output itself.

A situation where this type of operation is commonplace follows the validation of data input by a user. The JSP page often uses a JavaBean to validate the entries submitted on a user's form then redirects to another page according to the validity of the input data.

In the example below the JSP page uses a JavaBean called **bean3** that has a method called **isValid().** This will return a boolean value of **true** if the test is valid, or **false** if the test fails. The script on the JSP page uses the bean's **isValid()** method to apply a single **forward** action element that redirects to an appropriate page according to the returned boolean value.

forward.jsp

The page directive element in this example does not need a contentType attribute as there is no content output.

```
<%@ page language="java" %>

<jsp:useBean id="userData" class="mybeans.bean3" />

<% if(userData.isValid()) { %>

  <jsp:forward page="validpage.jsp" />

<% } else { %>

  <jsp:forward page="invalidpage.jsp" />

<% } %>
```

When the **isValid()** method returns **true**, control is passed to a page called **validpage.jsp** and this page is loaded into the browser. If the **isValid()** method returns **false**, control is passed to a page called **invalidpage.jsp** and that page is loaded into the browser.

invalidpage.jsp

```
<%@ page language="java"  contentType="text/html" %>

<html>
 <head><title>Data Validated</title></head>
 <body>
  <div style="border:double 3px silver">
  Your data entries are invalid - please retry.  </div>
 </body>
</html>
```

Notice that the address fields in the browser windows do not show the redirected location URIs.

validpage.jsp

```
<%@ page language="java"  contentType="text/html" %>

<html>
 <head><title>Data Validated</title></head>
 <body>
  <div style="border:double 3px silver">
  Your data entries are valid - thank you.  </div>
 </body>
</html>
```

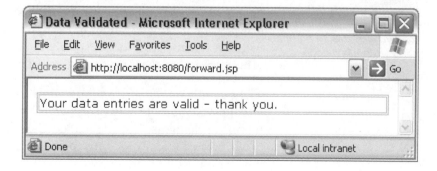

The plugin element

A Java applet is simply a Java class that is embedded into a Web page so it can be executed by the browser. Native support for Java in the browser software may vary so Sun Microsystems provide a free Java Runtime Environment (JRE) that can be integrated as a plug-in for Internet Explorer and Netscape browsers running on Windows, Linux and Solaris platforms. A complete list is available at `http://java.sun.com/products/plugin/index.html`.

The Java Plug-in allows applets to utilise all the latest Java features but the means of loading the plug-in into the browser sadly differs between Netscape and Internet Explorer. Netscape uses HTML <embed> elements for this purpose, whereas Internet Explorer uses <object> elements to do the job.

Happily, the JSP **plugin** action element provides a great solution to this problem. It examines the **User-Agent** request header, to identify the browser type, then inserts the appropriate HTML tags to load the plug-in into that particular browser.

A JSP **plugin** action element has three mandatory attributes that must always be included: Firstly, the **type** attribute must be set to either **applet** or **bean**. Next, the **code** attribute must specify the class name of the applet. Finally, the **codebase** attribute should state the absolute or relative location of the directory that contains the applet class file.

A pair of JSP **fallback** tags can optionally be nested inside the **plugin** tags to contain a default message that will be displayed if the plug-in cannot be loaded into the browser.

*JSP **param** elements can also be used with JSP **include** and **forward** elements to provide parameter information.*

Also a pair of JSP **params** (plural) tags can be nested within the **plugin** tags to contain one, or more JSP **param** (singular) elements that provide parameter values to the applet. Each **param** element will have a **name** attribute, to specify the parameter's name, and a **value** attribute to specify a value for that parameter.

The example on the opposite page uses an applet from Tomcat's **webapps\examples\jsp\plugin\applet** folder to demonstrate each of the above elements. The file named **Clock2.class** is copied into a newly created folder called **myapplets** which is a sub-directory of the Tomcat ROOT directory.

plugin.jsp

```
<%@ page language="java" contentType="text/html" %>
<html>
 <head><title>Plugin Element Demo</title></head>
 <body>
  <h3>Current time is :</h3>

  <jsp:plugin type="applet" code="Clock2.class"
    codebase="myapplets" width="160" height="150" >

  <jsp:fallback>
    Plugin tag OBJECT or EMBED not supported by browser.
  </jsp:fallback>

  <jsp:params>
    <jsp:param name="bgcolor" value="FFFFFF" />
    <jsp:param name="fgcolor1" value="000000" />
    <jsp:param name="fgcolor2" value="000000" />
  </jsp:params>

  </jsp:plugin>

 </body>
</html>
```

*This example sets parameter values for the applet's background and foreground colours. The size of the applet's area is also set by optional **width** and **height** attributes in the **plugin** element – a full list of optional attributes for the **plugin** element is given on the next page.*

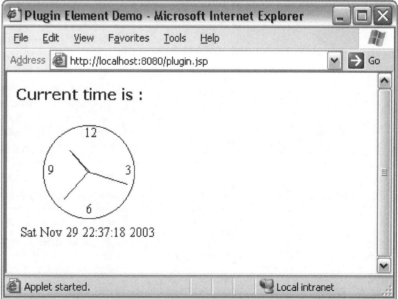

Optional plugin element attributes

In addition to the mandatory **type**, **codebase** and **code** attributes, which must appear in every JSP **plugin** action element, there are a number of other attributes which may optionally be included to provide further information to the applet.

The table below lists these optional attributes together with a brief description of how they may be used:

*The mandatory **type**, **codebase** and **code** attributes are demonstrated in the example on page 41.*

Attribute Name	Description
align	Aligns the applet area with acceptable values of either **top**, **middle** or **bottom**
archive	A comma-delimited list of URIs containing classes that may be used by an applet
height	Sets the height of the applet area with a value in pixels or a percentage
hspace	Specifies an amount in pixels of whitespace to appear at each side of the applet area
iepluginurl	States the URL location of the Java Plug-in for Internet Explorer browsers
jreversion	Identifies the version number of the JRE that is needed to run the applet
name	Assigns a name to the applet so it can be referenced by other applets on the page
nspluginurl	States the URL location of the Java Plug-in for Netscape browsers
title	Additional text to be displayed by the browser, such as an applet tool tip
vspace	Specifies an amount in pixels of whitespace to appear above and below the applet area
width	Sets the width of the applet area with a value in pixels or a percentage

A Java crash course

It is helpful to know the Java programming language in order to use some advanced features of JSP. This chapter provides an introduction to the basics of Java programming for those readers who are not already familiar with Java. It is not intended as a comprehensive guide to Java programming but is merely provided as an overview to aid in understanding some of the JSP examples given in this book.

Covers

Chapter Four

A first Java program

All Java programs start as text files that are later used to create Java **class** files – which are the actual runnable programs.

This means that Java programs can be written in any simple text editor such as Windows' Notepad application.

The Java code that is entered below into Notepad will generate the traditional first program output "Hello World".

Hello.java

```
Hello.java - Notepad
File  Edit  Format  View  Help
public class Hello
{
  public static void main (String args[ ])
  {
    System.out.println("Hello World");
  }
}
```

Programs are Java classes and the first line of this code defines the name of this program as **Hello**.

It is important to note that Java is a case-sensitive language where **Hello** and **hello** are seen as two entirely different programs.

Java program files are saved with their exact program name, matching character case, and with the file extension **.java**.

So the above program is saved as a file named **Hello.java**.

Create a new folder at C:\MyJava in which to save program files.

```
MyJava
File  Edit  View  Favorites  Tools  Help
Back    Search    Folders

Hello.java
```

Hello program analysed

The program code on the facing page can be broken down into three separate parts to understand it more clearly.

The Program Container

```
public class Hello { }
```

The program name is declared following the **public class** keywords and followed by a pair of curly brackets.

All of the program code that defines the Hello class will be contained within these curly brackets.

The Main Method

*All stand-alone Java programs must have a **main** method like the one shown here.*

```
public static void main (String[] args) { }
```

This fearsome looking line is the standard code that is used to define the starting point of nearly all Java programs.

It is used in a great many Java programs exactly as it appears above so this line may usefully be memorised.

The code declares a method named **main** that will contain the actual program instructions within its curly brackets.

Keywords **public static void** prefix the method name to define how it may be used and that no value is to be returned by this method.

The code **(String[] args)** is useful when passing String type values to the method for manipulation.

The Statement

```
System.out.println("Hello World");
```

Statements are actual instructions to perform program tasks and must always end with a semi-colon.

A method may contain many statements inside its curly brackets to form a statement block but, in this example, a single statement instructs the program to output a line of text.

Running the Hello program

Before a Java program can run it must first be compiled into a **class** file by the Java compiler. This is an application called **javac.exe** that is located in the **bin** folder of the Java SDK.

Remember that file names must be correctly capitalised.

To create a **class** file from a **java** source file, navigate from a command prompt to the directory containing the source file then at the prompt type **javac**, followed by a space. Next type the name of the file, including its file extension, and press the **enter** key.

If the compiler finds errors in the code it will halt and display a helpful report indicating the nature of the error. Typically errors are due to incorrect source code syntax or, where the compiler cannot find the source file, due to an incorrectly entered file name or path.

When the compilation succeeds, a new file is created in the current directory bearing the program name and the file extension **.class**. To run the program, type **java** at the command prompt, followed by a space and the name of the program without its file extension, then press the **enter** key.

The Hello program detailed on the previous page was saved in a folder at **C:\MyJava** and the process to compile and run this program is illustrated below:

Hello.class

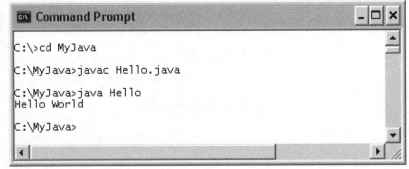

```
Command Prompt                                    _ □ ✕

C:\>cd MyJava

C:\MyJava>javac Hello.java

C:\MyJava>java Hello
Hello World

C:\MyJava>
```

When a program runs the Java interpreter reads the program **class** file and executes its instructions. In this case the statement contained in the program's main method will output the line of text "Hello World". Upon completion, focus returns to the standard command prompt.

Comments and backslash

It is useful, and good practice, when writing Java code to add comments that describe what each piece of code is doing. This makes the code easier to understand when it is revisited or when it is read by someone else.

The Java compiler sees any text between **//** and the end of that line as a single-line comment which it ignores. Also any text, on one or more lines, between **/*** and ***/** is ignored.

Spaces, tabs and new lines in the code are collectively known as **whitespace**. This too is ignored by the compiler so code may be formatted and indented to make it more readable.

The backslash character has a special meaning in strings. Inside quoted text strings **\n** will force a line-break in the output and **\t** will add a tab spacing to the output. It is also useful as **\"** will allow quotation marks to be used inside strings without prematurely terminating the string.

Here these features are added to the Hello program:

Hello.java
(modified)

Use \\ to
include a
backslash in a
quoted string.

```
/*
 * A First Java Program - With Added Features
 */
public class Hello
{
  public static void main (String[] args)
  {
    // add a new line, a tab and quotation marks
    System.out.println("\n\t\"Hello World\"");
  }
}
```

Hello.class
(modified)

```
Command Prompt                              _ □ ✕

C:\MyJava>javac Hello.java
C:\MyJava>java Hello

        "Hello World"

C:\MyJava>_
```

Variables and data types

A **variable** is simply a container in which a value may be stored for subsequent manipulation within a program. The stored value may be changed (varied) by the program as it executes its instructions.

Java is a strongly typed language that must specify when creating variables the type of data that may be stored inside.

To create a Java variable, and assign it a value, requires this syntax:

```
dataType variableName = value ;
```

A common type of Java variable is used to store text, as a string of characters, and is called a **String** data type.

The example code below creates a String variable called **str** that can be used by the program to refer to the stored text.

This program writes out the original variable value, then assigns a new value that is written out on the next line:

FirstVar.java

Text strings must always be surrounded by double quotes – to denote the string's start and finish.

```java
// demonstrate a String variable
public class FirstVar
{
  public static void main(String[] args)
  {
    String str = "First value";
    System.out.println(str);
    str = "Second value";
    System.out.println(str);
  }
}
```

FirstVar.class

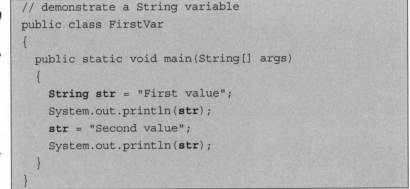

```
Command Prompt                          _ □ ✕

C:\MyJava>javac FirstVar.java

C:\MyJava>java FirstVar
First value
Second value

C:\MyJava>_
```

The full range of Java variable data types is listed in the table below together with a description of the type of data they may contain:

Keyword	Description of Data Type
char	A single Unicode character
String	A string of Unicode characters
int	An integer number from -2.14 billion to 2.14 billion
float	A floating-point number with a decimal point
boolean	A boolean value of true or false
byte	Integer number from -128 to 127
short	Integer number from -32,768 to 32,767
long	Positive or negative integer above 2.14 billion
double	A long floating-point number for double precision

*Characters assigned to a char variable should be enclosed in single quotes, not double quotes. Also note that the boolean **true** and **false** values are Java keywords that do not need to be enclosed by any quotes.*

Typical variable declarations for some of these types look like this:

```
char letter = 'M';
String str = "JSP in easy steps";
int number = "12345";
boolean flag = true;
```

When naming Java variables the name chosen should reflect the contents and must adhere to certain naming restrictions. All variable names should start with either a letter or the underscore character or a $ symbol. Numbers may be used elsewhere in the name but spaces are not allowed.

So **myVar1**, **_myVar** and **$myVar** are all valid names.

It is customary to begin variable names with a lowercase letter and class program names with an uppercase letter. If the variable name consists of more than one word they are joined together and all but the first word start in uppercase.

Arrays

An array is just a variable that can contain multiple values, unlike a regular variable that may only contain a single value.

An array declaration must first state its data type with the usual data type keywords but followed by square brackets to denote that it will be an array variable.

This is followed by a given name for the array that adheres to the normal naming conventions.

Values of the correct data type can then be assigned to the array as a comma-delimited list enclosed in curly brackets.

Remember that an array index starts at zero. So num[2] is a third element in an array, not the second.

The size of the array will be the length of the assigned list.

Stored values are indexed starting at zero and each value can be addressed by its index position in the list.

The program below first creates and initialises an array to store integers then outputs each of the stored values:

FirstArray.java

```java
public class FirstArray
{
  public static void main(String[] args)
  {
    int[] num= {100, 200, 300};

    System.out.println("First stored value is "+num[0]);
    System.out.println("Second stored value is"+num[1]);
    System.out.println("Third stored value is "+num[2]);
  }
}
```

FirstArray.class

```
Command Prompt                                    _ □ ×
C:\MyJava>javac FirstArray.java

C:\MyJava>java FirstArray
First stored value is 100
Second stored value is200
Third stored value is 300

C:\MyJava>_
```

Methods and statements

To call another method just use its name followed by any parameters in its following parentheses.

A statement in a Java program is a piece of code, terminated by a semi-colon, that performs a simple operation before the program moves on. Programs are typically separated into several methods, each containing a number of statements. Their statements are listed between a pair of curly brackets that follow the method's declaration.

The standard **main** method that appears in each program defines a String array called **args** in the parentheses following its name in the method declaration. This allows a number of text items to be passed to the method as a space-delimited list.

Other methods can receive values in the same manner by defining a data type and name in their declaration parentheses. Methods can also return values by changing the **void** keyword in their declaration to match the data type that is to be returned.

The first value passed to the program below is passed on to a second method for evaluation. An appropriate String is then returned to the first method which proceeds to display it.

FirstMethod.java

```java
public class FirstMethod
{
  public static void main(String[] args)
  {
    String str = evaluate(args[0]);
    System.out.println(str);
  }
  public static String evaluate(String entry)
  {
    if(entry.equals("Mike")) return "Hello Mike";
    else return "Sorry - I Do Not Recognise You";
  }
}
```

FirstMethod.class

```
C:\MyJava>java FirstMethod Mike McGrath
Hello Mike
```

Operators

Java statements can execute a variety of operations using the operators listed on these two pages to manipulate program values. Arithmetical operations can be performed with these operators:

Operator	Operation
+	Addition (and concatenates strings)
-	Subtraction
*	Multiplication
/	Division
%	Modulus
++	Increment
- -	Decrement

See page 58 for a loop example that uses the increment operator to count iterations and concatenates a string with the + operator.

These act much as expected but the **+** operator can also be used to concatenate two Strings into one single String. The modulus operator will divide a given first number by a second given number and return the remainder of the operation. This is most useful to determine if a number is odd or even. The increment and decrement operators alter the given value by 1 and are commonly used to count iterations of a loop.

Logical operators work on boolean values of **true** or **false**. The **&&** operator returns **true** only when both operands are **true**, whereas the **||** operator returns **true** when either of the two operands are **true**. The unary **!** operator returns the inverse value of the given operator, so if operand **A** is **true** then **!A** would return **false**.

Operator	Operation
&&	Logical AND
||	Logical OR
!	Logical NOT

It is important to regard the = operator to mean **assign**, rather than equals, to avoid confusion with the **==equality** operator. Other assignment operators, shown below, provide a shorthand method to combine arithmetical and assignment operations.

Operator	Example	Equivalent
=	a = b	a = b
+=	a += b	a = a + b
-=	a -= b	a = a - b
*=	a *= b	a = a * b
/=	a /= b	a = a / b
%=	a %= b	a = a % b

The comparison operators, listed in the table below, are used to compare the value of two operands and will return a boolean value of **true** or **false** according to the result of the comparison.

Operator	Comparative Test
==	Equality
!=	Inequality
>	Greater than
<	Less than
>=	Greater than or equal to
<=	Less than or equal to

See page 55 for an example of conditional branching.

Logical and comparison operators are most useful to branch the program along a particular route after testing a value. This is known as conditional branching and is an important programming technique to control program flow.

The conditional operator

The Java programmer's favourite test operator is probably the conditional operator. This first evaluates an expression for a **true** or **false** value then executes one of two given statements depending on the result of the evaluation.

The conditional operator has this syntax:

```
(test expression) ? if true do this : if false do this;
```

This operator is used to execute Java statements appropriate to the result of its conditional test.

The program below assigns an appropriate value to a String variable after determining if a tested number is odd or even:

Conditional.java

```
public class Conditional
{
  public static void main (String[] args)
  {
    int num1=1357, num2=2468;  // numbers to be tested
    String result;       // variable for result strings

    // test first number & assign string
    result= ( num1 % 2 !=0 ) ? "Odd" : "Even";
    System.out.println( num1+" is "+result );

    // test second number and assign string
    result= ( num2 % 2 !=0 ) ? "Odd" : "Even";
    System.out.println( num2+" is "+result );

  }
}
```

Notice here how the result variable is reused for efficiency.

Conditional.class

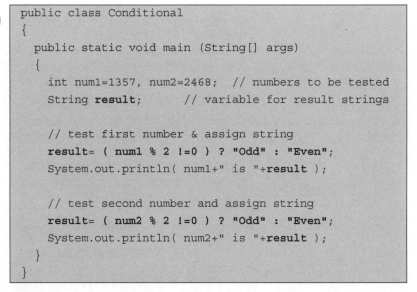

```
Command Prompt                                    _ □ ✕
C:\MyJava>javac Conditional.java

C:\MyJava>java Conditional
1357 is Odd
2468 is Even

C:\MyJava>_
```

Flow control

The flow of a Java program typically follows a series of conditional tests which determine the direction the program should follow. A most common test is performed using the Java **if** keyword to test an expression, enclosed in parentheses, for a **true** or **false** result. The statement following this type of test will only be executed when the expression is found to be **true**.

Remember to terminate each **if** *and* **else** *statement with a semi-colon.*

The Java **else** keyword can be used with an **if** statement to provide an alternative statement to be executed in the event that the tested expression is found to be **false**. Several expressions could be tested in this way until a **true** result executes the associated statement. It is important to note that any further code contained in the **if-else** block is ignored once the **true** statement has been executed.

In the simple example below a variable is tested to see if its value is equal to two. Once a **true** value is found its associated statement is executed, so the **if-else** block ends and the program moves on.

FirstBranch.java

```java
public class FirstBranch
{
  public static void main(String[] args)
  {
    int num=2;
    if(num==1) System.out.println("Num is 1");
    else
    if(num==2) System.out.println("Num is 2");
    else
    if(num==(1+1))System.out.println("Ignored text");
    else System.out.println("No match default text");
  }
}
```

FirstBranch.class

```
Command Prompt                                    _ □ ✕

C:\MyJava>javac FirstBranch.java

C:\MyJava>java FirstBranch
Num is 2

C:\MyJava>_
```

Switch statements

A **switch** statement performs the same function as an **if-else** statement that tests an expression against a given **case** value. When the result of the test is found to match the specified value then the code within that **case** statement is executed.

Each **case** statement should end with the Java **break** keyword to prevent the program continuing on to the next **case** statements. A final **default** statement can be included at the end of the block of **case** statements to specify code that should be executed in the event that the tested expression matches none of the **case** values.

In the example below the test expression is input from the command line when the program is run and assigned to a variable named **input**. The switch statement tests this for a match against two **case** values and provides a final **default** statement:

Switcher.java

The default statement at the end of the case block does not need to have a final break keyword.

```
public class Switcher
{
  public static void main(String[] args)
  {
    int input= Integer.parseInt(args[0]);
    switch( input )
    {
      case 1: System.out.print("Hello"); break;
      case 2: System.out.print("Goodbye"); break;
      default: System.out.print("Have a nice day");
    }
  }
}
```

Switcher.class

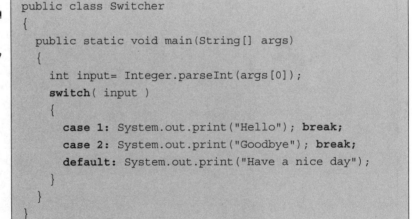

```
Command Prompt                                    _ □ ✕

C:\MyJava>javac Switcher.java

C:\MyJava>java Switcher 1
Hello
C:\MyJava>java Switcher 2
Goodbye
C:\MyJava>java Switcher 3
Have a nice day
C:\MyJava>_
```

Vectors

A **vector** is similar to an array but has greater flexibility that allows elements to be added, or removed, dynamically. This is more useful than array structures which always have a fixed size. Vectors are popular in JSP to provide a storage container for shopping basket items which can be added or removed dynamically.

The Java **vector** object has a method called **addElement()** that takes the value of a single element to add as its argument. Similarly the **removeElement()** method can remove an element.

All elements in a **vector** can be listed using its **elements()** method and assigned to an **Enumeration** object. A loop can then step through the list using the **Enumeration.nextElement()** method. The loop can be terminated by checking for a **false** return value from the **Enumeration.hasMoreElements()** method.

The Shopping Basket routine demonstrated in the final chapter of this book uses a vector to store items added by the user.

VectorDemo.java

The Vector class is a part of the java.util class which must be imported to make the Vector methods available.

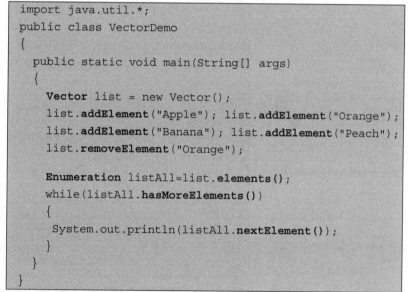

```java
import java.util.*;
public class VectorDemo
{
  public static void main(String[] args)
  {
    Vector list = new Vector();
    list.addElement("Apple"); list.addElement("Orange");
    list.addElement("Banana"); list.addElement("Peach");
    list.removeElement("Orange");

    Enumeration listAll=list.elements();
    while(listAll.hasMoreElements())
    {
     System.out.println(listAll.nextElement());
    }
  }
}
```

VectorDemo.class

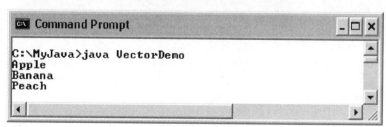

```
Command Prompt                              _ □ ×

C:\MyJava>java VectorDemo
Apple
Banana
Peach
```

Loops

A loop in a program will test an expression then execute a statement, or a block of statements, as long as the test is **true**. When the test is **false** the loop ends and the program moves on.

The most common type of loop found in Java programming uses the **for** keyword which has this syntax::

```
for (initialiser; test; increment ) { code to execute }
```

*Remember to terminate the initialiser and the test expression with a semi-colon in the **for** loop.*

The initialiser sets the starting value for a counter and is traditionally a variable named simply **i**. At each pass of the loop the test expression is evaluated to see if it remains **true**. If it does the counter is incremented and the statements are executed, otherwise, when the tested expression returns **false**, the loop ends at once.

The simple loop in the program below initialises a counter variable at one, then tests that its value is below six. While this remains **true** the value of the counter (**i**) is incremented by one and the statement code is executed on each pass. When the value of the counter reaches six the test becomes **false** and the loop ends.

FirstLoop.java

```java
public class FirstLoop
{
  public static void main(String[] args)
  {
    for(int i=1; i<6; i++)
    {
      System.out.println("This is iteration "+i);
    }
  }
}
```

FirstLoop.class

```
Command Prompt                                    _ □ ×
C:\MyJava>java FirstLoop
This is iteration 1
This is iteration 2
This is iteration 3
This is iteration 4
This is iteration 5

C:\MyJava>
```

Another loop uses the Java **while** keyword followed by an expression to be evaluated for a boolean value.

If the evaluation returns **true** then the code in the statement block will be executed. After the code has executed the test expression will again be evaluated and the loop will continue until the evaluation returns **false**.

An infinite loop will lock the program as it continues to run iterations.

The statement block must feature code that will affect the test expression in order to change the evaluation result to return **false**, otherwise an infinite loop will be created.

Note that if the test expression returns **false** when it is first evaluated the code in the statement block is never executed.

This program decrements two variable values on each iteration and decrements the counter until it reaches zero when the evaluation returns **false** and the loop ends.

WhileLoop.java

```java
public class WhileLoop
{
  public static void main(String[] args)
  {
    int a=30, b=15, i=3;
    while (i>0)
    {
      a -= 10; b -= 5; i--;
      System.out.println("A is "+a+"  B is "+b);
    }
  }
}
```

WhileLoop.class

```
Command Prompt                                    _ □ ✕

C:\MyJava>javac WhileLoop.java

C:\MyJava>java WhileLoop
A is 20  B is 10
A is 10  B is 5
A is 0  B is 0

C:\MyJava>
```

Objects and inheritance

Real-world objects are all around us and they each have attributes and behaviours that we can describe. Attributes depict features of an object and behaviours depict how the object may act. For instance, a car might be described with a body colour attribute of **blue** and a performance behaviour of **fast acceleration**. These features could be represented in Java programming by a Car class containing a **bodyColour** variable and a **performance()** method.

Java is said to be an object-oriented programming language because it makes extensive use of object attributes and behaviours to perform program tasks. Objects are created in Java by defining a class as a template from which copies, or **instances**, can be made. Most importantly, each **instance** of the class inherits attribute values and behaviours from its template. These can be customised in the **instance** of the class, by assigning new values to them, or the **instance** can make use of the inherited values.

The Java class shown below defines a simple template class that has four attributes, with initial values assigned, and one method that will display the value of each attribute in an output string. Notice that the static keyword is required to associate each feature with the class itself.

Car.java

```
public class Car
{
    static String marque = "Ford";
    static String model = "Mondeo";
    static String colour = "Red";
    static String doors = "Four";

    static void specs()
    {
        String str = "\n\tThis car is a "+marque+" "+model;
        str += "\n\tIt is finished in "+colour;
        str += "\n\tand it has "+doors+ " doors";
        System.out.println(str);
    }
}
```

A template class need not include a main method itself because the **instances** of this class will each define their own main method.

The main method of the CarInstance program, shown below, declares an object named **myCar** of type **Car** that creates an **instance** of the Car class using the **new Car()** constructor.

The attribute **myCar.colour** *is not assigned a new value so it inherits its* **Red** *value from the template.*

This new **myCar** object inherits the attributes and methods of the Car class, together with their assigned values. These can be referenced using dot syntax to append an attribute or method name after the **myCar** object name. The CarInstance program assigns new values to some of the **instance** attributes then calls the **specs()** method to display the **instance** values in a string.

CarInstance.java

```
public class CarInstance
{
  public static void main(String[] args)
  {
    Car myCar = new Car();
    myCar.marque = "Porsche";
    myCar.model = "911 Carrera";
    myCar.doors = "Two";
    myCar.specs();
  }
}
```

CarInstance.class

```
Command Prompt                                    _ □ ✕

C:\MyJava>java CarInstance

        This car is a Porsche 911 Carrera
        It is finished in Red
        and it has Two doors

C:\MyJava>_
```

This ability to easily use pre-defined classes in this way is a hugely important feature of Java programming. The Java SDK provides a multitude of pre-defined classes of tried and tested code that are used to create new Java programs. This saves on development time and helps to ensure the robustness of any new Java program. These classes are also available to JavaServer Pages.

Java classes in JSP

The classes most frequently used with JSP are mainly concerned with Strings of text. An instance of the **String** class (a String object) can be created and initialised using the **new** constructor keyword:

```
String greeting = new String("Welcome");
```

The String class has methods named **equals()**, **equalsIgnoreCase()**, **concat()** and **trim()** which are useful when handling Strings:

```
// Test a string with and without regard to case
greeting.equals("Welcome"); // returns true
greeting.equals("welcome"); // returns false, but...
greeting.equalsIgnoreCase("welcome"); // returns true

// concatenate a second string with the original
greeting=greeting.concat(" to Java ");

// trim the trailing space from the string
greeting=greeting.trim(); // now "Welcome to Java"
```

For more on Java programming, consider referring to 'Java2 in easy steps':

Variables cannot be changed to a different data type but their values can be transferred to another variable of a different data type in a procedure known as **casting**. The String class's **valueOf()** method can cast a numeric data type value into a String variable.

Numeric values stored in **String** variables must be **cast** into appropriate numeric type variables before arithmetical operations can be performed on them. The **Integer** class has a **parseInt()** method to cast **String** values into **int** variables and the **Float** class has a **parseFloat()** method to cast **String** values into float variables:

*Notice that float values must be suffixed with a **F** or **f** to denote that they should be treated as float types – otherwise they will be treated as double data types.*

```
int integerNumber=100;        // cast int to String...
String stringNumber = String.valueOf(integerNumber);

String strNumber = "200";      // cast String to int...
int intNum = Integer.parseInt(strNumber);

float floatNumber = 3.142F; // cast float to String...
String stringNum = String.valueOf(floatNumber);

String strFloat = "98.6";    // cast String to float...
float floatNum = Float.parseFloat(strFloat);
```

Implicit JSP objects

This chapter provides an overview of the nine Java objects that are built into the JSP specification. Some of their more common methods are demonstrated here and further methods of these objects are used in other examples later in this book.

Covers

Chapter Five

The request object

The JSP **request** object has a variety of methods to access the information contained in the request header sent from a browser when requesting a JSP page. These can reveal details about request parameters, attributes and cookies and are examined in detail in various individual examples later in this book.

The JSP page shown below demonstrates how a variety of the **request** methods can display common request header information:

reqinfo.jsp

```
<%@ page language="java" contentType="text/html" %>
<html>
  <head> <title>Request Header Info</title> </head>
  <body bgcolor="white">
  <ul>
  <li/>Request Method:     <%= request.getMethod() %>
  <li/>Request URI:     <%= request.getRequestURI() %>
  <li/>Request Protocol: <%= request.getProtocol() %>
  <li/>Server Name:     <%= request.getServerName() %>
  <li/>Server Port:     <%= request.getServerPort() %>
  <li/>Remote Address:  <%= request.getRemoteAddr() %>
  <li/>Browser: <%= request.getHeader("User-Agent") %>
  </ul>
  </body>
</html>
```

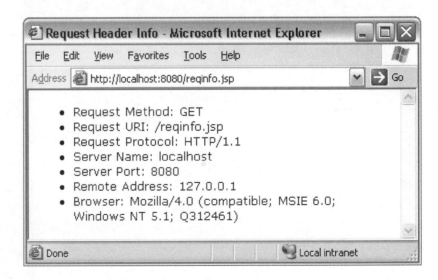

The response object

The **response** object relates to the response headers that are sent to the browser from the server along with the current page. It has methods to specify header information and status code. For instance, **response.sendError(500)** will report an internal server error to the browser. Also **response** methods can be used for session tracking and to add cookies to the users browser cache.

The JSP page below demonstrates how **response** methods can set the content type, and display some common header information:

response.jsp

```
<%@ page language="java" %>
<% response.setContentType("text/html"); %>
Buffer Size:<%= response.getBufferSize() %> bytes <br/>
Character Encoding:<%= response.getCharacterEncoding()%>
<br/> Locale:<%= response.getLocale() %>
```

You can prevent the browser adding the page into its cache memory by setting the header with response.addHeader("Cache-Control" "no-cache");

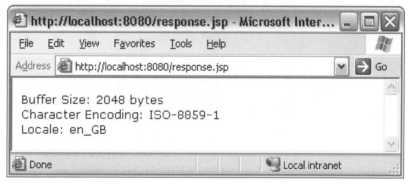

See page 108 to see how the response object's encodeURL() method is used for session tracking.

It is sometimes useful to have the server redirect a user to another URL and the **response** object provides a **sendRedirect()** method for this very purpose. The location of the new URL must be stated as the method's argument, between quotes within its parentheses, and must be a full absolute address, as shown in this example:

```
<%@ page language="java" %>

<%-- redirect the user to another.html --%>

<% response.sendRedirect(
            "http://localhost:8080/another.html"); %>
```

The application object

The JSP **application** object is used to hold references to other objects that may be accessed by multiple users. This could be a common value such as a database connection or any other fixed attribute that may be useful across the application. **setAttribute()** and **getAttribute()** methods of the **application** object allow easy storage and retrieval of common values.

Additionally the **application** object has a **log()** method that allows information to be written to the log file for that application. This is normally found in Tomcat's **logs** directory and is given a name by the server something like **localhost_log** and the current date.

Notice that the returned value attribute is cast into a suitable String variable.

In the example below an attribute named **user** is assigned a value before control is passed on. The second page is able to retrieve this attribute's value and write it both on the page and in the log file.

app1.jsp

```
<%@ page language="java" %>
<% application.setAttribute("user","David McGrath"); %>
<jsp:forward page="app2.jsp" />
```

app2.jsp

```
<%@ page language="java" contentType="text/html" %>
<% String attrib =
String.valueOf( application.getAttribute("user") ); %>
Hello <%= attrib %>
<% application.log( "User:"+attrib ); %>
```

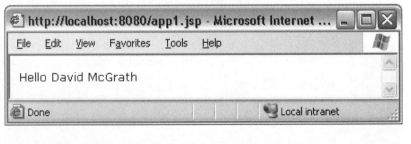

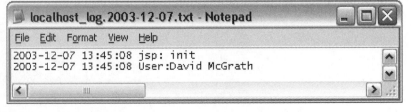

The session object

When a JSP page is opened in a browser a unique session identity is allocated for each user accessing that application. This information is contained in the JSP **session** object.

Like the **application** object on the opposite page, the **session** object also has **setAttribute()** and **getAttribute()** methods but their attributes will only be available for the current session user, not all users of the application.

The session identity is created dynamically as a hexadecimal number that can be retrieved using the **session.getId()** method.

A session can remain open even when the user moves to a new URL but is terminated when their browser is closed. In order to avoid another user of the browser gaining access to that session, perhaps when the user leaves their desk without closing their browser, it is best to positively terminate the session using the **session** object's **invalidate()** method. This effectively provides a log out procedure for the application and bars access to any **session** attributes.

The simple example below displays the **session** identity, then terminates the session and confirms that the session is ended:

session.jsp

```
<%@ page language="java" contentType="text/html" %>
Session: <%= session.getId() %> <hr/>
<% session.invalidate(); %>
Session: <% if(session.getId() != null)
              System.out.println(session.getId());
          else System.out.println("Session ended"); %>
```

When a session has ended a call to the session.getId() method will return a null value.

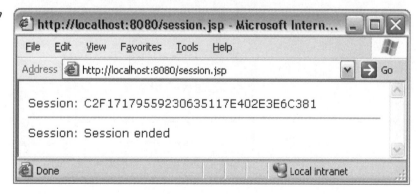

The out object

The JSP **out** object handles text output from the JSP application. Its **print()** method is useful to add text to the body of the response, from the server to the browser, as an alternative to simply using template text and JSP action elements. The **print()** method will output the text string set as its argument, enclosed in quotes, between its parentheses.

The **out** object also has methods to query the page buffer. If the **page** directive attribute **autoflush** is set to true (the default), the buffer will be automatically cleared when it becomes full to avoid an error occurring.

In the JSP page below the application demonstrates the **out.print()** method then establishes some page buffer information:

out.jsp

```
<%@ page language="java" contentType="text/html" %>

<%-- print a heading --%>
<% out.print("<h3>JSP BufferInformation</h3>"); %>

<%-- display the page buffer size --%>
Buffer:<%= out.getBufferSize() %> bytes <br/>

<%-- display the AutoFlush setting --%>
AutoFlush: <%= out.isAutoFlush() %> <br/>

<%-- display the free page buffer space --%>
Remaining buffer: <%= out.getRemaining() %> bytes
```

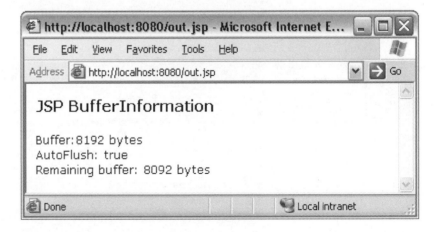

The exception object

The JSP **exception** object contains information about errors that occur at runtime and is only available on pages that are specified to be an error page. This requires that a page directive attribute called **isErrorPage** should be assigned a **true** value.

An original JSP page can designate an error page, to be used in the event that a runtime error occurs, by including a page directive with an **errorPage** attribute specifying the URL of the desired error page.

The **exception** object has a **getMessage()** method that delivers a concise description of the cause of the error. In this example the original page creates an error by attempting to get the value of a session attribute after the session has terminated. The specified error page then displays the error message to the user:

error.jsp

```
<%@ page language="java" contentType="text/html" %>
<%@ page errorPage="errorpage.jsp" %>
<% session.setAttribute("user","Andrew McGrath"); %>
User: <%= String.valueOf(session.getAttribute("user"))%>
<% session.invalidate(); %>
User: <%= String.valueOf(session.getAttribute("user"))%>
```

errorpage.jsp

```
<%@ page language="java" contentType="text/html" %>
<%@ page isErrorPage="true" %>
<html> <head> <title>Error Page Demo</title> </head>
<body> <h3>Ooops! - this error has occurred:</h3>
<blockquote> <%= exception.getMessage() %></blockquote>
</body></html>
```

See Chapter 7 for more on error handling and debugging.

More implicit objects

In addition to the six implicit objects described already throughout this chapter the JSP specification provides three further implicit objects that are used behind the scenes to deliver JSP pages. They are seldom, if ever, used for scripting purposes but are outlined below for completeness.

The config object

This object is used to contain information that is to be passed to the servlet or JSP page when it is initialised. These include parameters used to initialise the page whose names can be listed with a **getInitParameterNames()** method. The String value of each parameter can be returned by a **getInitParameter()** method that takes a parameter name as its sole argument.

The page object

This is an instance of the **Object** class that is a part of the standard Java library and simply creates the page as a unique object. There is no reason to reference this object directly.

The pageContext object

This object is an instance of a Java class that contains information relating to the accessibility of the JSP page features and attributes. The accessibility information controls the scope of how they may be used by other JSP classes so the servlet may be portable. A unique instance of this object is created by each page request. The **pageContext** object has many methods to perform tasks which are more easily undertaken using other JSP object methods. So, in practice, **pageContext** methods do not need to be called directly.

That completes the initial overview of the JSP implicit objects. Many of their methods are recreated in JSP actions which allow the non-programmer to ignore their existence. Knowledge of how these objects can be used may prove beneficial, however, when creating exciting JSP pages.

If you are interested in reading the full specification for each of the nine JSP implicit methods you can download the complete JSP documentation from Sun Microsystems. This is comprehensive but may seem over-facing to those who are new to the Java programming language or to JavaServer Pages.

Download the full JSP documentation from Sun at `http://java.sun.com/products/jsp/download.html`

Scriptlets

This chapter demonstrates JSP scripting. It starts by giving a simple scriptlet example then compares how the scriptlet may be rewritten to use a JavaBean component. Further examples illustrate how to identify the user's browser and how JSP can handle user input.

Covers

Chapter Six

A conditional Java welcome

JSP elements can be used to determine which parts of the template text should be included in the final generated HTML page by performing a conditional test.

The example below first creates an instance of the Java **Date** class that is part of the **java.util** library of classes. This object is named **now** and is displayed on the page to indicate the date and time when it was created. **Date** objects have a method named **getHours()** that returns just the hour value from the full date.

Comparisons can be made against the hour in an **if-else** statement block by enclosing the Java code within <% ... %> tags. Only the template text between the tags where a **true** condition is found will be used in the generated page.

welcome1.jsp

```
<%@ page language="java" contentType="text/html" %>

<html> <head> <title>Welcome Scriptlet</title> </head>
<body bgcolor="white">

<% java.util.Date now = new java.util.Date(); %>
Current date &amp; time: <%= now %>

<span style="font:bold 28pt black">

<% if(now.getHours() < 12) { %> Good Morning!
<% } else if(now.getHours() < 17) { %> Good Afternoon!
<% } else { %> Good Evening! <% } %>

</span> </body> </html>
```

For more on Java flow control see page 55.

A conditional JavaBean welcome

The conditional Welcome scriptlet on the facing page can be rewritten in JSP to use a JavaBean component.

The **jsp:useBean** action element creates an instance of the Java class that is specified by its **class** attribute. The name of the class instance is determined by the name assigned to its **id** attribute.

The example below creates an instance of the **java.util.Date** class named **now**, in a similar manner to the previous example. The **getHours()** method of this class instance is used in just the same way but this approach is more elegant.

welcome2.jsp

```
<%@ page language="java" contentType="text/html" %>

<html> <head> <title>Welcome Scriptlet</title> </head>
<body bgcolor="white">

<jsp:useBean id="now" class="java.util.Date" />

Current date &amp; time: <%= now %>

<span style="font:bold 28pt black">

<% if(now.getHours() < 12) { %> Good Morning!
<% } else if(now.getHours() < 17) { %> Good Afternoon!
<% } else { %> Good Evening! <% } %>

</span> </body> </html>
```

Details about writing custom JavaBeans can be found in Chapter 10.

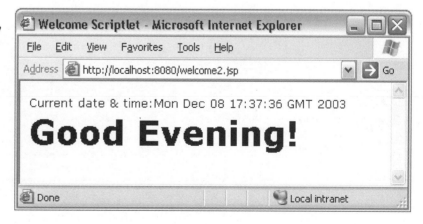

Identifying the browser

Requests from a browser to the server include a header called **User-Agent** that contains information identifying the browser. This information can be retrieved by the JSP **request.getHeader()** method and examined so that a response appropriate to the browser's capabilities may be sent from the server.

The Java **String.indexOf()** method can be used to examine the **User-Agent** string for a match to a string specified as its argument. Internet Explorer browsers will match the string **MSIE**, Netscape browsers will match the string **Mozilla** and Opera browsers will normally match the string **Opera**.

The JSP page below checks the type of browser then displays an appropriate message followed by the full **User-Agent** string:

browser.jsp

```
<%@ page language="java" contentType="text/html" %>
<html>
<head> <title>Browser Check Demo</title> </head>
<body bgcolor="white">

<% String userAgent = request.getHeader("User-Agent");
   String browser = "Unknown Browser";

   if( userAgent.indexOf("MSIE") != -1)
   { browser = "Internet Explorer"; }
   else
   if( userAgent.indexOf("Mozilla") != -1)
   { browser = "Netscape"; }
   else
   if( userAgent.indexOf("Opera") != -1)
   { browser = "Opera"; }
%>

<b>Welcome <%= browser %> User</b> <br>

User Agent: <%= userAgent %>

</body> </html>
```

The User-Agent string includes information regarding the user's platform.

The illustrations shown on the opposite page show the above page in a variety of Web browsers. These are all made on the same system despite the differing appearance of the **User-Agent** string.

...cont'd

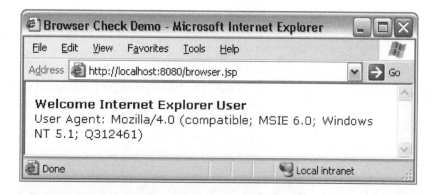

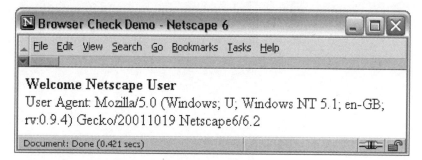

Opera has an option allowing users to set the browser identity to represent Mozilla or MSIE.

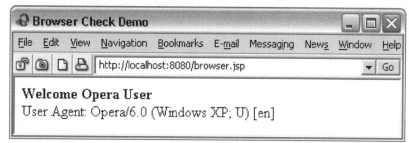

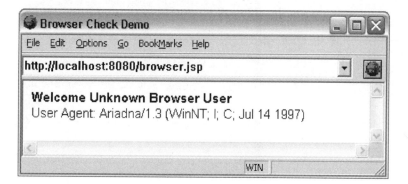

Sending form data

Submitting HTML forms with JSP sends the form data to the server as request parameters in the usual style of key/value pairs. The key name is the name assigned to the input field by the **name** attribute of the HTML **input** element. The parameter value can be retrieved by the **request.getParameter()** method which takes the parameter key as its argument and returns the associated value.

The **action** attribute in this example specifies a JSP page that will handle the data entered by the user when the form is submitted.

sendform1.jsp

```
<%@ page language="java" contentType="text/html" %>
<html>
<head> <title>Send Form Demo</title> </head>
<body bgcolor="white">
<div style="width:250px;text-align:right">

<form action="sendform2.jsp">
Name: <input type="text" name="user" value=""> <br/>
Country: <input type="text" name="land" value=""><br/>
Email: <input type="text" name="addr" value=""> <br/>
<input type="submit" value="Submit">
</form>

</div> </body> </html>
```

This form is completed by the user and is ready for submission:

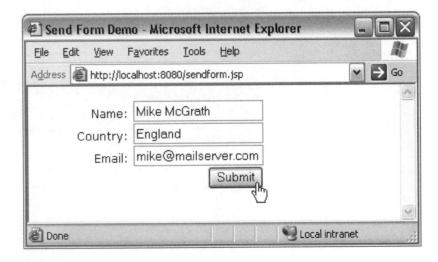

The JSP page to handle the submitted data seeks the parameter keys individually for the input fields named **user**, **land** and **addr**, using the **request.getParameter()** method.

sendform2.jsp

```
<%@ page language="java" contentType="text/html" %>
<html>
<head><title>Send Form Demo</title><?head>
<body bgcolor="white">

<h3>Welcome
<%
    if(!request.getParameter("user").equals("") )
    { out.print( request.getParameter("user") ); } %>

from
<%
    if(!request.getParameter("land").equals("") )
    { out.print( request.getParameter("land") ); } %>
</h3>

More details will be sent to:
<%
    if(!request.getParameter("addr").equals("") )
    { out.print( request.getParameter("addr") ); } %>

</body></html>
```

Notice the use of a ! operator to include printed output only when the field is NOT an empty string – when the user has entered some text into the text box.

If the parameter value associated with each key is not an empty string it is included in the response sent back to the browser.

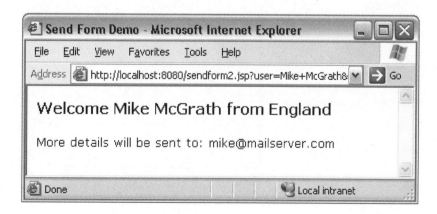

Form data loops

Forms that submit data from a number of input fields bearing the same name, such as a list of selections, form a parameter key/value pair. The key is the name assigned to the input fields by the **name** attribute in the HTML **input** element. The **value** of each input field is listed as an array of items associated with that single key.

The JSP **request.getParameterValues()** method can be used to retrieve the list of submitted values by specifying the key name as the argument between its parentheses. This returns an array of the data values that can be assigned to a **String[]** array variable.

Array index numbering starts at zero, not one.

Each of the items contained in the array can be addressed using the array name and their index position between square brackets, for instance **myArray[1]** addresses the second item in an array named **myArray**. The total length of the array can be discovered with its **length** property, such as **myArray.length**.

The JSP page below is called **selectform1.jsp** and contains a list of **checkbox input** elements that all share the same name of **cities**. The form's **action** attribute specifies that the submission be handled by another JSP page named **selectform2.jsp** that is listed on the opposite page.

selectform1.jsp

Source code for selectform1.jsp is identical to that listed on page 81 except the action attribute assigns selectform2.jsp to handle the submission in this case.

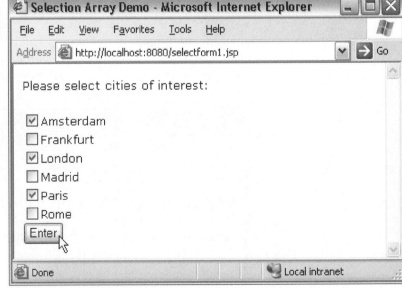

...cont'd

It is common for a JSP response to list all the selected data that has been submitted from a form by looping through the value array. Typically this is a Java **for** loop that starts at index item zero and continues until reaching the end of the array.

The page below assigns the data submitted from the form opposite to a String array called **pick**. It first checks that the array actually exists then loops through each item in the array to display all of the values selected by the user.

selectform2.jsp

For more on scripting loops in Java – see page 58.

```jsp
<%@ page language="java" contentType="text/html" %>
<html>
<head><title>Selection Array Demo</title></head>
<body bgcolor="white">

<% String[] pick = request.getParameterValues("cities");

    if(pick != null && pick.length != 0) { %>

Thank you for registering your interest in these cities:
<ul>

  <% for(int i=0; i < pick.length; i++)
  { out.print("<li>"+pick[i]); } %>

<% } %>

</ul>
</body></html>
```

Mirror submitted data

It is often desirable to mirror the form input made by a user in a response page as a confirmation of their selections. The form can be simply repeated with JSP elements marking the selected items.

Multiple selection values submitted as an array, with a single key, can be compared against the response form elements so that JSP can mark those which match.

To avoid repeating the code to check each element individually it is better to create a separate Java class which can then be included in the JSP page with **page import** directive.

The **ThisArray.java** example below is added to Tomcat's **classes** folder where it will be found automatically by the server. This class provides a method called **contains** that takes two arguments stating the name of the array to search, and the name of the value to seek. It first checks that the array exists then loops through each of the array items looking for a match to the specified value. When the value is found the method returns **true**, otherwise it returns **false**.

ThisArray.java

*Notice the use of the Java **break** keyword to immediately halt the loop when a match is found.*

```
public class ThisArray
{
public static boolean contains(String[] key, String val)
{
  boolean exists = false;
  if (key == null || val == null) { return false; }
  for (int i = 0; i < key.length; i++)
  {
    if (val.equals( key[i])) { exists = true; break; }
  }
  return exists;
}
}
```

The JSP page **mirroform1.jsp** listed opposite is almost identical to the **selectform1.jsp** page shown on page 78 but its **action** attribute is changed to specify that **mirrorform2.jsp** should now handle the submission. The **mirrorform2.jsp** page imports the **ThisArray** class to make its **contains method** available to compare the selected values. Its full code is listed on page 82 and an illustration of the response page sent to the browser is shown on page 83.

...cont'd

mirrorform1.jsp

```
<%@ page language="java" contentType="text/html" %>
<html>
<head> <title>Mirror Selection Demo</title> </head>
<body bgcolor="white">
Please select cities of interest:<br/>

<form action="mirrorform2.jsp">
<input type="checkbox" name="cities"
                value="Amsterdam">Amsterdam<br/>
<input type="checkbox" name="cities"
                value="Frankfurt">Frankfurt<br/>
<input type="checkbox" name="cities"
                value="London">London<br/>
<input type="checkbox" name="cities"
                value="Madrid">Madrid<br/>
<input type="checkbox" name="cities"
                value="Paris">Paris<br/>
<input type="checkbox" name="cities"
                value="Rome">Rome<br/>
<input type="submit" value="Enter">
</form> </body> </html>
```

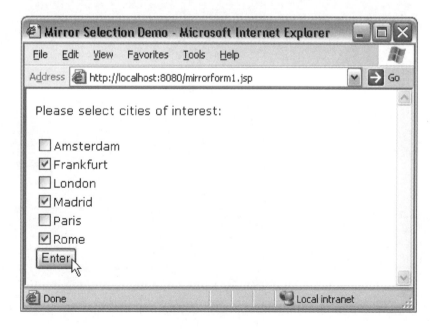

mirrorform2.jsp

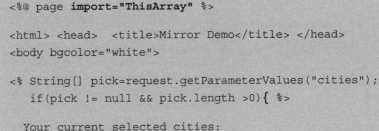

The JSP elements use the conditional operator to insert checked for matched selections – for more on the conditional operator see page 54.

```jsp
<%@ page language="java" contentType="text/html" %>

<%@ page import="ThisArray" %>

<html> <head>  <title>Mirror Demo</title> </head>
<body bgcolor="white">

<% String[] pick=request.getParameterValues("cities");
   if(pick != null && pick.length >0){ %>

 Your current selected cities:

 <form action="process.jsp">
 <input type="checkbox" name="cities" value="Amsterdam"
 <%= ThisArray.contains(pick,"Amsterdam")? "checked":""
 %> >Amsterdam<br/>

 <input type="checkbox" name="cities" value="Frankfurt"
 <%= ThisArray.contains(pick,"Frankfurt")? "checked":""
 %> >Frankfurt<br/>

 <input type="checkbox" name="cities" value="London"
 <%= ThisArray.contains(pick,"London")? "checked":""
 %> >London<br/>

 <input type="checkbox" name="cities" value="Madrid"
 <%= ThisArray.contains(pick,"Madrid")? "checked":""
 %> >Madrid<br/>

 <input type="checkbox" name="cities" value="Paris"
 <%= ThisArray.contains(pick,"Paris")? "checked":""
 %> >Paris<br/>

 <input type="checkbox" name="cities" value="Rome"
 <%= ThisArray.contains(pick,"Rome")? "checked":""
 %> >Rome<br/>

 Press the <input type="submit" value="Proceed"> button
 to continue

 </form>

<% } %>

</body> </html>
```

...cont'd

The import directive simply makes its specified Java class accessible to the JSP processor.

The **import page** directive in **mirrorform2.jsp** causes the **ThisArray.java** file to be compiled to create a **ThisArray.class** file by Tomcat.

The response page sent to the browser reproduces the form on the original page and recreates the user's selections by checking the checkboxes matching the original selections:

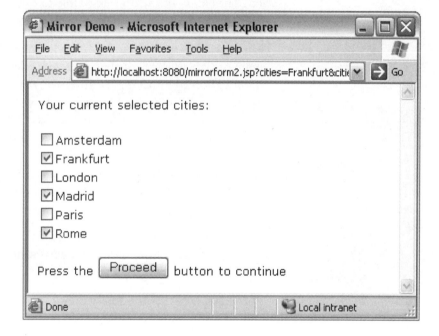

At this stage the user may change selections by returning to the original page with the browser's **back** key, making new selections, then once more pressing the **Enter** button to submit the new selections to **mirrorform2.jsp**.

If the user is happy with these selections he or she may progress to the next stage of the application by pressing the **Proceed** button. This will submit the form selections to another JSP page called **process.jsp** to continue onward as required by the application.

Why different tag styles?

JSP **action** elements, such as **<jsp:useBean>**, use the XML-style notation that will be familiar if you know the XML language.

On the other hand, JSP directive and scripting elements like **<%@ directive %>** and **<%= expression %>**, use **<% %>** notation that is unrecognised in XML.

As XML is set to be the future standard way to write all markup languages it would seem reasonable to question why the modern XML notation is not used for all JSP elements.

For more on the XML language please refer to 'XML in easy steps':

The main reason to avoid XML-style notation for JSP scripting elements is that some of the characters contained in scripting code are not allowed in XML. For instance, the less-than **<** character and the greater-than **>** character represent the beginning and end of tags in the XML language. If JSP used XML-style notation for its scripting elements these characters would need to be manually encoded to avoid confusing the XML parser. Otherwise an error would be generated. This requirement would necessarily create code that was less-easily readable and more prone to errors.

It is also useful to retain the **<% %>** notation for many developers who are familiar with **<%@ directive %>**, **<% code %>**, **<%= expression %>** and **<%! declaration %>** because they may have used the same tags in Microsoft's Active Server Pages (ASP).

The JSP specification actually does mention XML elements for JSP scripting tags, such as **<jsp:directive>**, **<jsp:scriptlet>** and **<jsp:expression>** although these are designed for use only by software tools that can automatically generate complete JSP pages.

These XML elements are really only useful to represent a view of a JSP page as a XML document. In this case the software tool must ensure that the entire syntax of the page is compliant to XML standards and this infers that the tool must also encode all special characters to avoid the problems mentioned above.

Unless you are creating JSP pages as XML documents you should currently only use **<% %>** notation for JSP scripting elements.

Error handling

This chapter examines some of the errors that will inevitably occur during the development of a JSP application. It explores syntax and design errors, then discusses debugging and how to handle runtime errors.

Covers

Chapter Seven

Element syntax errors

The most simple type of error is one that you will probably have already encountered if you have been working through the examples in this book. Simply mis-typing an element name or attribute name, or just omitting a single character can create a syntax error where the JSP processor cannot read your code. When the browser calls a page that contains a syntax error Tomcat reports the nature of the error in an alarming-looking manner.

The simple JSP page shown below contains three typos which each cause a syntax error. The first is the omission of the **%** character at the end of the **page directive** element:

syntaxerror.jsp

```
<%@ page language="java" contentType="text/html" >
<jsp:useBean id="time" class="java.util.Date" >
<html>
<head><title>Syntax Error Demo</title></head>
<body>
The time is
<jsp:getProperty ame="time" property="hours" /> :
<jsp:getProperty name="time" property="minutes" />
</body> </html>
```

Tomcat detects the first error and immediately stops parsing the code. The error causes a Java exception which is pinpointed in the error report, partly shown opposite, that is sent to the browser.

The long list at the end of the error report is called a **stack trace** and is useful to describe the error to Java programmers. Of more immediate interest to JSP developers is the first line under the exception heading which identifies the error. In this case it reads: **syntaxerror.jsp(0,49) Unterminated <%@ tag**.

This helpful information details the file name, line number and character position of the offending error, then states that the element tag is not correctly closed.

After adding the missing **%** to the page directive element Tomcat reports the second syntax error when the page is reloaded into the browser. This time the **jsp:useBean** element is found to be not closed properly because the closing tag's **/** character has been omitted. Tomcat reports the error on the first line under the exception heading like this: **syntaxerror.jsp(14,7) useBean tag must begin and end in the same physical file**. This rather more cryptic message means that the indicated element starts out as XML so it should be closed in the XML fashion.

After adding the missing **/** to the **jsp:useBean** element Tomcat reports the third syntax error when the page is reloaded into the browser. This is a typing error that has omitted the letter **n** from the **name** attribute in the first **jsp:getProperty** element.

Tomcat reports the resulting exception with this message: **syntaxerror.jsp(9,0) getProperty: Mandatory attribute name missing**. This does not let you know that the attribute is misspelt but simply states that a required attribute is missing. Correcting the spelling rectifies all the syntax errors so the JSP page can now function properly.

These are examples of some fairly typical syntax errors that are easily resolved with the help of the Tomcat exception reports.

Apache Tomcat/4.0.1 - HTTP Status 500 - Internal Server Error

type Exception report

message Internal Server Error

description The server encountered an internal error (Internal Server Error) that prevented it from fulfilling this request.

exception

```
org.apache.jasper.compiler.ParseException:
syntaxerror.jsp(14,7) useBean tag must begin and
end in the same physical file
at
org.apache.jasper.compiler.Parser$Bean.accept(Parser.java:657)
```

Scriptlet syntax errors

The error messages generated by Tomcat when a scripting syntax error is found are often more difficult to interpret than those for element syntax errors. This is because element syntax errors are discovered when the JSP processor is converting the JSP page into Java servlet code, whereas scripting errors are not discovered until the Java compiler begins to compile that code into a servlet class.

It is important to note, therefore, that a scripting syntax error report refers to the error's location within the generated servlet code, rather than its location in the original JSP code. This sometimes makes it difficult to identify the nature of an error.

The JSP page below omits the final closing curly bracket from the **if-else** statement block thus creating the error report opposite :

scripterror.jsp

```
<%@ page language="java" contentType="text/html" %>
<jsp:useBean id="time" class="java.util.Date" />
<html>
<head><title>Scripting Error Demo</title></head>
<body>
<% if(time.getHours() < 12) { %> Good Morning
<% }else if(time.getHours() <17) { %> Good Afternoon
<% }else{ %> Good Evening
</body> </html>
```

The single error is reported as 3 errors because it creates three errors in the Java compiler, the first two relating to an incomplete **try-catch** statement block. This does not appear in the original JSP code but has been generated as servlet code from the JSP scriptlet.

A **try** keyword allows Java code to attempt to execute a number of contained statements. It provides a means to deal with possible exceptions using a **catch** keyword. Optionally it may also specify a final statement to execute with a **finally** keyword. None of these are required in the JSP scriptlet but are explained here in order to help understand the generated error report.

The final reported error is more helpful in identifying the cause of the problem as it explicitly states that a **}** character was expected, but not found. Unless the scriptlet is unusually complex it is a simple matter to check the scriptlet code for the missing character.

The line numbers in the error report refer to lines in the servlet code – not the original JSP code.

exception

```
org.apache.jasper.JasperException: Unable to
compile class for JSP
C:\Tomcat\jakarta-tomcat
4.0.1\work\localhost\_\scripterror$jsp.java:108:
'catch' without 'try'.
        } catch (Throwable t) {
        ^

C:\Tomcat\jakarta-tomcat
4.0.1\work\localhost\_\scripterror$jsp.java:116:
'try' without 'catch' or 'finally'.
}
^

C:\Tomcat\jakarta-tomcat
4.0.1\work\localhost\_\scripterror$jsp.java:116:
'}' expected.
}
^
3 errors
```

The generated servlet source code can be examined with a text editor and can be found at the location stated in the report.

The omission of curly brackets, especially in nested statement blocks, is a particularly common scripting syntax error. Another one is the omission of closing brackets in nested statements. For instance, it is easy to make a syntax error like this one:

```
<% if(requestHeader("User-Agent").indexOf("MSIE")!=-1 %>
     You're using Microsoft Internet Explorer
```

In this case the Tomcat error report is more helpful and can pinpoint the precise location of the error because the missing closing bracket is required to make a valid Java expression:

```
Generated servlet error: C:\Tomcat\jakarta-tomcat-
4.0.1\work\localhost\_\scripterror$jsp.java:115:
')' expected.
if(requestHeader("User-Agent").indexOf("MSIE")!=-1
                                                  ^
1 error
```

Debugging scriptlet errors

Logic errors contained in JSP scriptlets can be identified by adding debugging code to temporarily display variable values at each stage of the program.

The JSP page below contains a scriptlet that should display a message appropriate to the user's browser type:

browsermsg.jsp

```
<%@ page language="java" contentType="text/html" %>
<html> <head> <title>Browser Message</title></head>
<body bgcolor="white">

<% String browser = request.getHeader("User-Agent"); %>

<% if( browser.indexOf("Mozilla") != -1) %>
Welcome Netscape User

<% else if( browser.indexOf("MSIE") != -1) %>
Welcome Internet Explorer User

<% else if( browser.indexOf("Opera") != -1) %>
Welcome Opera User

</body> </html>
```

This scriptlet works as intended in Netscape or Opera browsers:

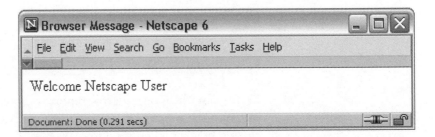

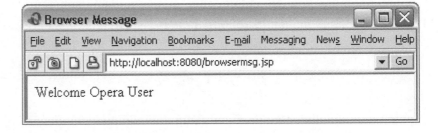

When the scriptlet is run in Internet Explorer, however, it incorrectly displays the message intended only for Netscape. A temporary line of code can be added after the scriptlet to debug this problem by displaying the **browser** variable's value.

```
<%= "<hr>BROWSER: "+ browser +"<hr>" %>
```

Now when the JSP page is run in the browser it also reveals the browser's **User Agent** header information that is stored in the **browser** variable:

Always include horizontal rules over and under debugging code – this added prominence will help you remember to delete it later.

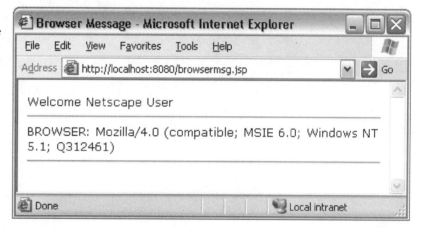

The displayed variable value makes it apparent that the problem is caused because the Internet Explorer **User-Agent** header also contains the string **Mozilla** that is used to check for Netscape.

The solution to the problem is to rearrange the scriptlet so that it tests for the string **MSIE** first, to establish if the user has Internet Explorer, before seeking the **Mozilla string** that tests for Netscape.

In a scriptlet where a variable value undergoes a whole series of changes, such as in an arithmetical function, it is a good idea to add code to display its value at each step of the program.

Once the scriptlet has been debugged don't forget to remove any of the code that has been used to resolve logic errors.

Handling runtime errors

Runtime errors are created when external input does not match that anticipated by the JSP application. This might, perhaps, be because a database is unavailable or, more typically, because a user enters data of a type not expected by the application. For instance, a scriptlet may expect to receive a parameter value representing an integer value, but the user inputs a floating point value instead.

The following example demonstrates this problem. The JSP application expects to receive input from the user that can be cast into an **int** type variable. However, if the user enters non-integer values, or zero, the scriptlet throws an exception to the error page assigned in the second **page** directive.

errorlog.jsp

Input entered by the user is retrieved, when the form is submitted, by the request.getParameter() method – see page 76.

```
<%@ page language="java" contentType="text/html" %>
<%@ page errorPage="errorpagelog.jsp" %>
<html>
<head> <title> Division Form </title> </head>
<body>
<form action="errorlog.jsp">
Number:
<input type="text" size="2" name="number" value="">
Divide by:
<input type="text" size="2" name="divider" value="">
<input type="submit" value="GO">
<input type="text" name="result" readonly
value="
<% String number =  request.getParameter("number");
   String divider =  request.getParameter("divider");
   if( number!=null && !number.equals("") )
   {
     if( divider !=null  && !divider.equals("") )
     {
       int num = Integer.parseInt(number);
       int div = Integer.parseInt(divider);
       out.print( num +" / "+div+" = "+ (num/div) );
     }
   }
%>
">
</form> </body> </html>
```

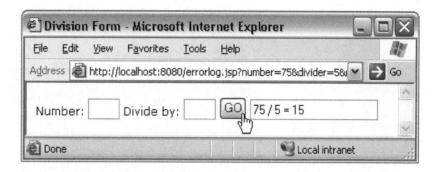

This application displays a division sum input by the user together with its result when submitted, as seen above. Its code checks to see that both fields have received some kind of input then proceeds to execute the division calculation. If either of the fields have received input that cannot be cast into an **int** type variable an exception is thrown to the error page shown below.

The example illustrates the resulting output from the error page if a user attempts to divide an integer value by zero:

errorpagelog.jsp

Error details are written to the log file using the application.log() method – see page 66.

```jsp
<%@ page language="java" contentType="text/html" %>
<%@ page isErrorPage="true" %>
<% String errorMsg = exception.getMessage(); %>

<html> <head> <title>Error Logging Demo</title> </head>
<body>
Error: <%= errorMsg %> <br>
<% application.log(errorMsg); %>
Error details have been automatically logged.
</body></html>
```

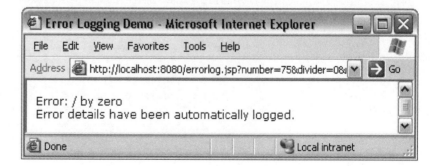

Java IDE debugging

Most scriptlet coding is relatively simple so tracking down errors is usually not too troublesome. If the scriptlet code is reaching a level of complexity that makes debugging difficult you should consider moving some of the code into JavaBeans or custom actions.

Visual Age for Java is available from IBM at `http://www-4.ibm.com/software/ad/vajava` *and a JBuilder 30-day trial can be downloaded from Borland at* `www.borland.com/jbuilder.`

Like other compiled programming languages, such as C, C++ and C#, Java has several excellent Integrated Development Environment (IDE) software applications to aid the developer. The IDEs include Visual Age for Java from IBM, and JBuilder from Macromedia, which each offer an integral debugger to help resolve coding errors. With these you can step through a Java program to a pre-defined breakpoint in order to identify any errors. They are not required for simple JSP pages but can be helpful to debug JavaBean code in more advanced JSP applications.

This illustration shows the JBuilder IDE and the beginning of a JSP-generated servlet code.

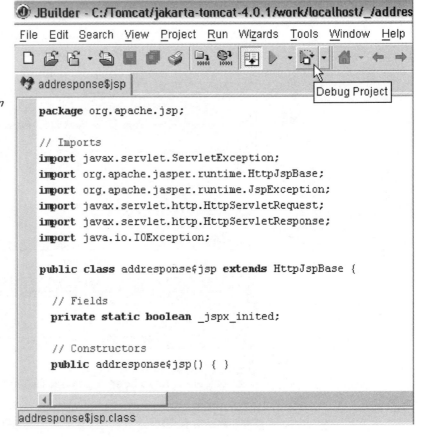

Data control

This chapter illustrates how to pass control and data between multiple JSP pages. It demonstrates how this may be used to validate user input sent to the server and how to limit the accessibility of data by setting its scope range.

Covers

Chapter Eight

Separating display and logic

A main aim of JSP is to separate request processing and output display. This is achieved using different JSP pages to handle the processing logic and the display response. Each of the pages in the application must be able to pass data along to the next page.

The diagram below illustrates a multiple page application that is detailed fully later in this chapter. An initial request to **datainput.jsp** displays a form to gather user input. The form submission is handled by the **datacheck.jsp** logic page that uses a JavaBean to validate the input. It will **forward** the user back to the original page if the input is incomplete or invalid, and provide a message describing how to proceed. When the input is entirely valid the **datacheck.jsp** logic page will **forward** the user to the **datavalid.jsp** page which acknowledges the valid input.

Only **datainput.jsp** and **datavalid.jsp** can send a response to the browser – **datacheck.jsp** provides no HTML output but only provides processing logic.

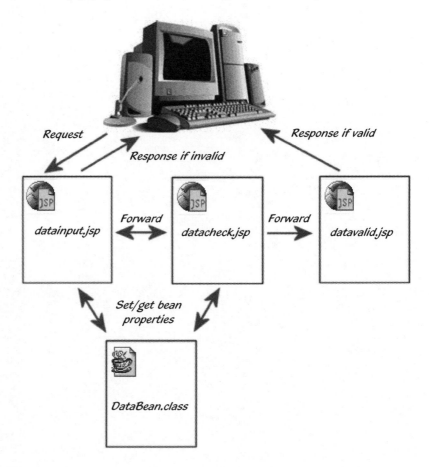

Setting scope for shared data

Most real-world JSP applications have multiple pages which often need access to common information. For instance, when one page retrieves requested data and another displays it they need a way to pass the data from one page to the next. Additionally, some pages need to have access to information to be shared among multiple pages, requests and all users, such as database connection details.

The **scope** of shared data can be set as **page**, **request**, **session** or **application**, to specify how long it is available and whether it is accessible by just one user or by all users of that application. Data with the default **page** scope is only accessible from scriptlets on that page but **request** scope allows the data to be available to all pages processing that request. Data shared by multiple requests from the same user can be available if set as **session** scope, whereas **application** scope data can be shared by all users of the application.

Only use the application scope when you are certain that all users of the application will need access to the shared data.

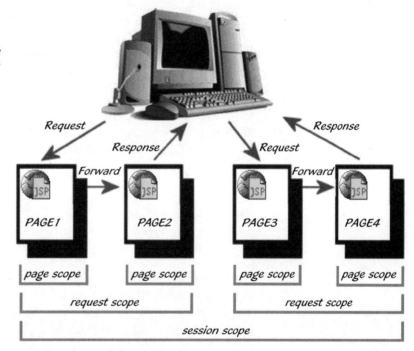

The illustration above depicts the extent of the restrictive scopes. Most frequently used are the **session** scope, and the **request** scope that is demonstrated in the ensuing example in this chapter.

Sharing request data

The multiple-page model described on page 96 is demonstrated in action over the next few pages showing each step of the process.

Display the form

The first JSP page in this multiple-page application is called **datainput.jsp** and its job is to display a form that requires two input fields to be completed by the user.

In order to share data the page first creates an instance, named **Data**, of a JavaBean called **DataBean**. The actual bean is a Java **class** file located in the **mybeans** sub-directory of Tomcat's **classes** folder. It contains properties called **userName** and **emailAddr** which are used to store the user's entries.

The accessibility of the data is specified by setting the **scope** attribute of the **jsp:useBean** element to **request**. This makes the stored data available to each page of the application for multiple requests by the same user.

When this form is submitted the JSP application will check to see that both fields have been completed. Additionally, it will check that the **Email** field entry contains an **@** character and a **dot** to verify that the format appears to be that of an email address.

DataBean has a method called **getFillFormMsg()** that displays the default message **Please enter name & email address** when the input fields contain no text.

The form's action attribute assigns the second JSP page, called **datacheck.jsp**, to handle the data when the form is submitted. This page does not directly generate any HTML output but provides the logic to process the submission.

The form's input fields are named **userName** and **emailAddr** to match the **DataBean** properties where the input will be stored. These values can be retrieved from the bean using its **getUserName()** and **getEmailAddr()** methods. Each of these methods are called to assign their stored data value to the **value** attribute of the relevant HTML **input** element. If the properties are empty these methods will assign an empty string as the value.

The full source code of **datainput.jsp** is listed on the opposite page.

datainput.jsp

Notice that the scope for this bean is set to request – to be available for multiple requests from any single user.

```jsp
<%@ page language="java" contentType="text/html" %>
<html>
<head> <title>Data Input Form</title> </head>
<body bgcolor="white">
<div style="width:250px;text-align:right">

<jsp:useBean id="Data"
            class="mybeans.DataBean" scope="request" />

<%-- Output any invalid entries --%>
<%= Data.getFillFormMsg() %>

<%-- Output form with any submitted valid values --%>
<form action="datacheck.jsp" method="post">

Name:<input type="text" name="userName"
            value="<%= Data.getUserName() %>" > <br/>

Email:<input type="text" name="emailAddr"
            value="<%= Data.getEmailAddr() %>" > <br/>
<input type="submit">
</form>

</div> </body> </html>
```

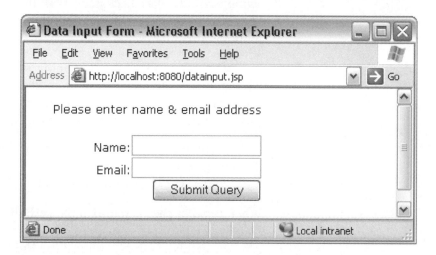

The example continues on the next page where the user enters some text and submits the form to be processed...

Submit the form

To demonstrate the submission of data which fails validation, the user input in the illustration below supplies an invalid email address format and omits the user name completely:

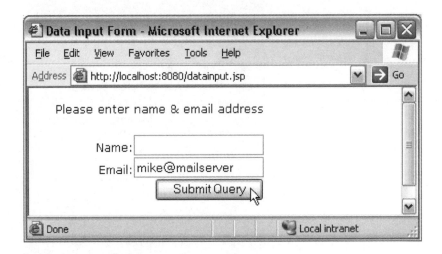

Process the form

When the form is submitted the JSP page specified by the form's **action** attribute, **datacheck.jsp**, sets all the properties in the **DataBean** so they are assigned the values that were entered into the input fields by the user.

It then processes a scriptlet containing an **if-else** statement. The test condition calls a **DataBean** method named **isValid()** that will return **true** when the entries are complete and meet all the validation rules, otherwise it will return **false**.

If the form input is valid the scriptlet will **forward** the user onto the final page but if the form is incomplete, or the entries invalid, the scriptlet will **forward** the user back to the first page to retry.

When the first page is reloaded the **getFillFormMsg()** method of **DataBean** will display a message advising the user how to proceed. Also the **getUserName()** and **getEmailAddr()** methods will insert any valid value into the relevant input field so that the user need not re-enter the data in that field.

datacheck.jsp

Notice how the **jsp:setProperty** *action element assigns a wild card * to its property attribute — to set all properties when the bean instance is created.*

```
<%@ page language="java" %>

<jsp:useBean id="Data" scope="request"
                      class="mybeans.DataBean" >
  <jsp:setProperty name="Data" property="*" />
</jsp:useBean>

<% if (Data.isValid()) { %>
  <jsp:forward page="datavalid.jsp" />
<% } else { %>
  <jsp:forward page="datainput.jsp" />
<% } %>
```

With the invalid and incomplete input data shown opposite, the scriptlet reloads **datainput.jsp**, which now looks like this:

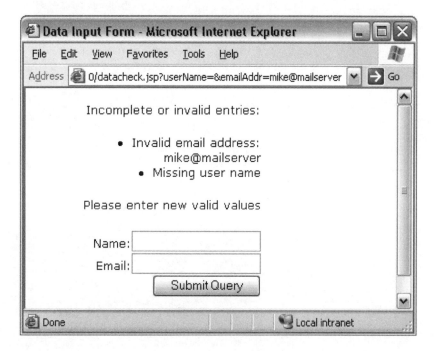

In this case the user has not managed to enter any valid data so the input fields remain empty. Armed with the information displayed by the **getFillFormMsg()** method, the user is able to complete the form correctly and re-submit the form, as we can see overleaf...

Acknowledge valid input

When the form below is submitted the required data is complete and valid so the processing page, **datacheck.jsp**, forwards the user to the final page in this application **datavalid.jsp**. This page simply acknowledges that the data input by the user was validated correctly.

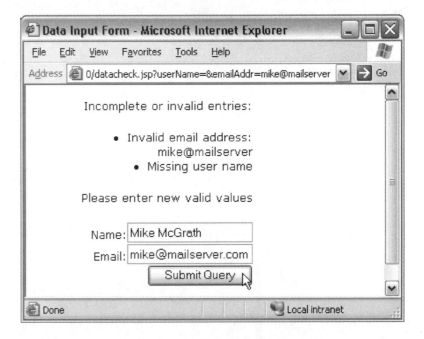

datavalid.jsp

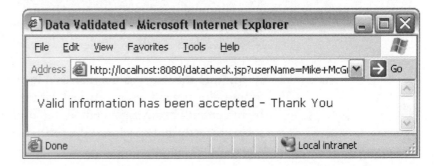

```
<html> <head> <title>Data Validated</title> </head>
<body bgcolor="white">
Valid information has been accepted - Thank You
</body> </html>
```

Sharing application data

The data in the example starting on page 98 is shared in the **request** scope because it is specific to the current user so should not be accessible to any other users. In complete contrast to this is data that is shared in the **application** scope so that it is available to any user at any time.

Typically data that is to be shared universally relates to server information, such as database connections, details about currently logged-in users and cache objects which avoid unnecessarily repeating database lookups.

This common information is shared in the **application** scope and is represented in the illustration below:

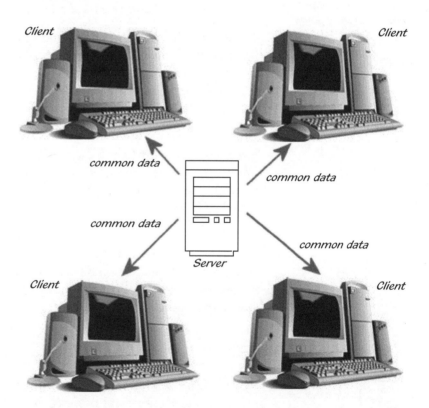

In contrast to **application** scope, **session** scope is described on the next page and the example on page 107 demonstrates both **application** scope and **session** scope to contrast their differences.

Sharing session data

The Hypertext Transfer Protocol (HTTP) handles requests and responses between the Web browser and the server without any memory of the process – once it has sent a response the server remains unaware of the event. This means that when the same browser sends another request the server is unable to recognise that it may be related to the previous one.

The grace period allowed by Tomcat can be adjusted from its default value of 30 minutes by changing a session-timeout value in the web.xml file in Tomcat's conf directory.

When the pages being delivered are simply static Web pages, which display text and graphics, their relationship is unimportant. However, it becomes important when the pages being delivered are part of an interactive application. In this situation it is vital that the process can share data across different pages in the application. For instance, user input electing preferences must be accessible by other pages so the user need not repeatedly state those preferences.

JSP resolves this problem by sending a piece of information called a **session ID** to the browser when it makes an initial request. The browser then includes this **session ID** information when it makes any subsequent requests to the server so that it can be uniquely identified. This allows the server to determine that certain requests are related because they all bear the same **session ID** information.

A **session** is started when the server receives the first request from a browser and it is terminated either when the user closes the browser, when the application explicitly ends the session or after a period of inactivity from that browser. The precise length of this grace period can be configured on the server.

The server stores **session** data in memory using the **session ID** to associate it with the **session** object for that browser. Data saved in the **session** scope is available to the same browser at any time during that session.

```
http://localhost:8080/sessioninfo.jsp;jsessionid=
C0B4E0569494B9471451D0B1B1E80973
```

See page 108 for more on URL rewriting and session tracking.

By default the **session ID** is normally transferred invisibly by JSP using cookies on the client browser. Alternatively the **sessionID** can be explicitly transferred employing a technique called URL rewriting to automatically append the **session ID** onto URLs – so they look like the illustration above. This method maintains the **sessionID** where cookies are not available on the client browser.

The provision of JSP **session ID** identifiers allows multiple browsers to use the same JSP application simultaneously with each storing their own unique data for use by that application. This identification process is depicted in the illustration below:

The session ID is automatically allocated to the browser when it is sent the response to its first request.

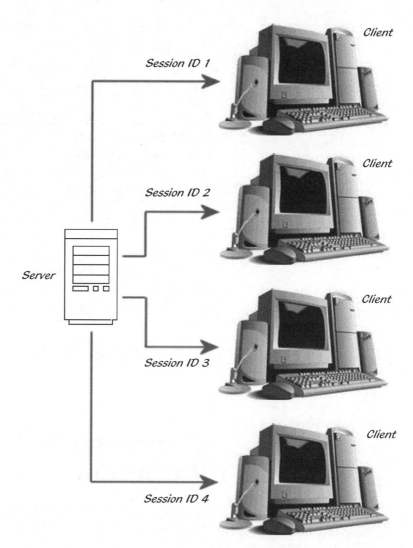

The **session** scope is demonstrated in an example on the next page that contrasts its functionality with the **application** scope.

Counting page views

This example uses a JavaBean that stores in memory the number of times a URI is visited and its **getHitNumber()** method returns the current total. It demonstrates here the different effect of using the bean in the **session** and **application** scopes:

hitcounter.jsp

```
<%@ page language="java" contentType="text/html" %>
<html> <head> <title>Hit Counter Demo</title> </head>
<body bgcolor="white"> <h1>Hit Counter</h1>

<% String URI = request.getRequestURI(); %>

<jsp:useBean id="sessionCounter" scope="session"
class="mybeans.HitBean" />
This page has been viewed
<%= sessionCounter.getHitNumber(URI) %> times <br/>
by this browser in the current session. <hr/>

<jsp:useBean id="applicationCounter" scope="application"
class="mybeans.HitBean" />
This page has been viewed a total of
<%= applicationCounter.getHitNumber(URI) %> times <br/>
by all users since the application was started.
</body> </html>
```

The page has been reloaded three times to bring the total number of hits to four in this illustration.

Both counters initially start at one and reloading the page increments each counter by one. Opening a second browser to view the same page reveals that the session counter again starts at one but the application counter displays the overall number of page viewings. Reloading the first browser now increments the session counter total by one but the application counter total by two, to include the page viewed in the other browser.

The Netscape browser receives a new session ID so the session counter starts at one. The application counter increments the last total of four by adding another one.

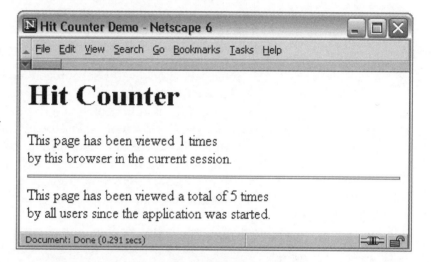

Reloading Internet Explorer adds one to its previous session total of four and increments the last total, seen in the Netscape browser, by adding one.

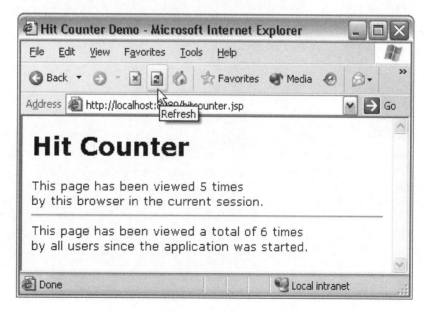

Session tracking

The session ID can be set explicitly using cookies, or by encoding the URLs contained in all hyperlinks on the page employing a technique called **URL rewriting**. It is recommended that the cookie method is not used as some users do not allow cookies to be stored on their computers and new smaller devices that can now access the Internet may not have the ability to store cookies.

The **response.encodeURL()** method is used for URL rewriting in JSP and takes the address of the target as its argument. This allocates a **session ID** that is passed to the next page when the user follows the link and the server extracts this to identify the session.

In the example below, the **session.getCreationTime()** is used to display the time when the session was created. As this method returns a value in milliseconds, a scriptlet is added to convert the returned value into a more friendly date format. When the hyperlink is followed, the **session ID** value is automatically passed onto the next page with a parameter key called **jsessionid**. This can be retrieved from the **request** header, after the initial request, with the **request.getRequestedSessionId()** method.

sessioninfo1.jsp

The JSP page sessioninfo2.jsp contains the same code as sessioninfo1.jsp except that the page number differs in the heading, and the hyperlink targets sessioninfo1.jsp.

```
<%@ page language="java" contentType="text/html"%>
<html>
<head> <title>Session Info</title></head>
<body> <h1>This is page 1 </h1>

Session Creation Time: <%= session.getCreationTime() %>
(milliseconds elapsed since 1st January 1970 00:00 GMT)
<br/><br/>

Session Created:
<% java.util.Date startedAt = new java.util.Date();
   startedAt.setTime( session.getCreationTime() );
   out.print( startedAt ); %>    <br/><br/>

Session ID: <%= request.getRequestedSessionId() %>
<br/><br/>

<a href="<%= response.encodeURL("sessioninfo2.jsp")%> ">
Go to page 2</a>

</body> </html>
```

The session ID is not set when the first request is made but subsequently following the links always displays the same details.

Notice in this illustration that the session ID is included in the address field with the jsessionid key.

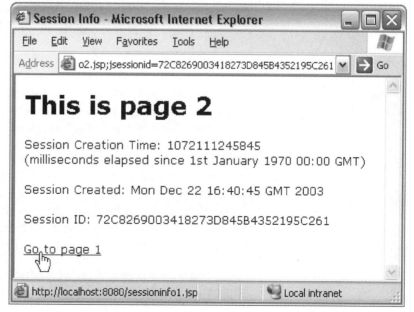

Considering server memory

Each piece of data stored in the **application** and **session** scope occupies memory on the server and a popular site can require considerable memory to store all these objects.

The amount of memory needed for the application scope can be calculated because each object is specified only once.

The amount of memory needed for the session scope, on the other hand, is determined by the number of specified objects multiplied by the number of concurrent sessions.

Imagine a popular site with an average of 3,000 users per hour, storing an average of 10 Kb of data per session, and with a default timeout for each session of 30 minutes. At any point there could be 3,000 active sessions plus a further 3,000 sessions that have not yet timed out. This makes a total of 6,000 concurrent sessions requiring around 60Mb of memory.

A memory requirement of 60Mb is not excessive in itself but this example illustrates how memory requirements grow with the number of concurrent sessions.

It is helpful in reducing the memory requirement to make judicious use of the **session** scope by only placing in it objects that absolutely need to be unique to that session. Place all other objects wherever possible in the **application** scope.

The JSP session.invalidate() method is used in the example on page 67.

Another way to reduce the memory needed on the server is to provide a way to end the session explicitly using the **session.invalidate()** method. Typically this can be used when a final task is completed, such as when a form is submitted, or with a logout function when the user has finished with the application.

It is also sometimes worth reducing the timeout period from its 30 minutes default value to reduce the number of session objects being stored after the users have left the application. For instance, if it is uncommon for users to return to an application after 15 minutes the timeout period could safely be reduced to 15 minutes thus potentially reducing the total memory requirement by 25%.

These concerns may not arise with many applications but it is helpful to consider memory needs when using the **session** scope.

User recognition

This chapter demonstrates some of the ways to customize page content so that it appears appropriate to the user's expectations. Examples illustrate language formatting, date formatting and number formatting, and cookies are used to store preferences.

Covers

Chapter Nine

Finding the user's location

The request header sent from the browser contains information about the user's location in a **Locale** object. This comprises two standard abbreviations describing the language and country of origin. The language is given in lowercase, such as **en**, for English, or **fr** for French, whereas the country is shown in uppercase, such as **GB** for Great Britain, or **US** for the United States.

The **Locale** information can be discovered using the **request.getLocale()** method. This method returns the abbreviations linked together with an underscore, like **en_GB**.

All the Java Locale methods are made available to the page by importing the java.util package in a page directive.

The language and country abbreviations can be retrieved separately with **Locale.getLanguage()** and **Locale.getCountry()** methods. Perhaps more usefully, the **Locale.getDisplayLanguage()** and **Locale.getDisplayCountry()** provide fuller descriptions.

The scriptlet in the example below displays the **Locale** information details then writes a message in the appropriate language:

locale.jsp

```jsp
<%@ page language="java" contentType="text/html" %>
<%@ page import="java.util.*" %>

<html> <head> <title>User Location</title></head>
<body bgcolor="white"> <ul>

<% Locale here = request.getLocale();
 out.print( "<li>Locale: "+ here );
 out.print("<li>Language Code: "+ here.getLanguage());
 out.print("<li>Language:"+ here.getDisplayLanguage());
 out.print("<li>Country Code: "+ here.getCountry());
 out.print("<li>Country: "+ here.getDisplayCountry());
%>

</ul> <h3>
<% if( here.getLanguage().equals("de") ) { %>
 Willkommen zu dieser Seite
<% } else if( here.getLanguage().equals("fr") ) { %>
 Bienvenue à cette page
<% } else { %>
 Welcome to this page
<% } %>
</h3> </body> </html>
```

...cont'd

 All abbreviation language codes are defined in ISO-639 and can be found at `www.id3.org/ iso639-2.html`. *All country codes are defined in ISO-3166 available at* `www.id3. org/iso3166.html`.

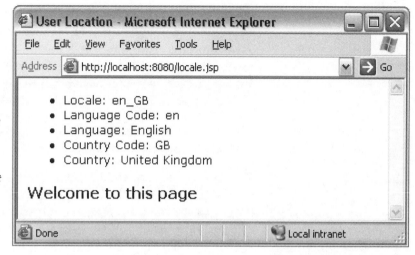

The JSP page opposite produces the output shown above for a user located in the UK. For demonstration purposes the **Locale** can be set to represent another country, say France, by assigning a **new Locale()** to the **here variable** instead of using the **request.getLocale()** method, like this:

```
Locale here = new Locale("fr","FR");
```

So now the same JSP page produces the output below that would be appropriate to a user located in France:

 The Locale information could be used to forward the user to a page in their own language with a jsp:forward action element.

Formatting dates

Dates should be displayed carefully to ensure that the correct date information is seen by the user because some countries reverse the day and month from the British format (DD-MM-YY) to the American format (MM-DD-YY). This means that 3/5 represents 3rd May to UK users but March 5th to US users. For this reason it is advisable to display dates using month names where possible.

All the Java DateFormat methods are made available to the page by importing the java.text package in a page directive. The java.util package is also imported to make the Date and Locale classes available.

The user's location can first be discovered with the JSP **request.getLocale()** method, as described on the previous pages.

The date can be formatted to appear in the user's local style with the Java **DateFormat** class. This has a **getTimeInstance()** method, to get just the time, a **getDateTimeInstance()** method to get the date and time, and a **getDateInstance()** method to get just the date.

Optionally, the **getDateInstance()** method may have two arguments to specify required formatting of the date.

The first argument may set the general style of the date to be either long, medium or short. These can be specified as integer values 1, 2 or 3, or by using these constants:

*   **DateFormat.LONG**, (as 1) – producing 25 December 2003

*   **DateFormat.MEDIUM**, (as 2) – producing 25-Dec-03

*   **DateFormat.SHORT**, (as 3) – producing 25/12/03

The second argument may set the internationalised style of the date by specifying a **Locale**.

When the desired formatting has been specified the date can be translated into a String by the **DateFormat.format()** method.

In the JSP page shown opposite the scriptlet first assigns the current date to a **Date** variable called **today** and the user's locale to a **Locale** variable called **here**. A **DateFormat** variable called **df** is then assigned a date instance that specifies a long general style that should be internationalised for the current **Locale**. This is finally used to format the current date in the output.

Further examples in the scriptlet set the **Locale** to other countries to demonstrate how the date appears in their local style.

...cont'd

dateformat.jsp

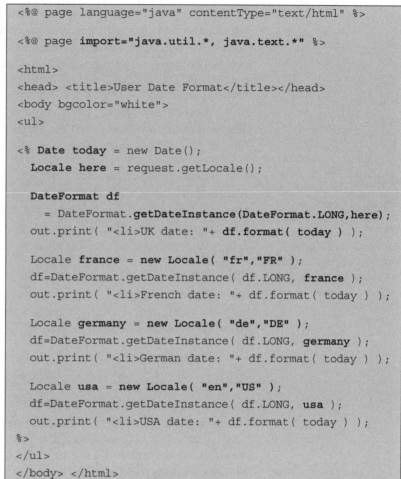

```
<%@ page language="java" contentType="text/html" %>

<%@ page import="java.util.*, java.text.*" %>

<html>
<head> <title>User Date Format</title></head>
<body bgcolor="white">
<ul>

<% Date today = new Date();
   Locale here = request.getLocale();

   DateFormat df
     = DateFormat.getDateInstance(DateFormat.LONG,here);
   out.print( "<li>UK date: "+ df.format( today ) );

   Locale france = new Locale( "fr","FR" );
   df=DateFormat.getDateInstance( df.LONG, france );
   out.print( "<li>French date: "+ df.format( today ) );

   Locale germany = new Locale( "de","DE" );
   df=DateFormat.getDateInstance( df.LONG, germany );
   out.print( "<li>German date: "+ df.format( today ) );

   Locale usa = new Locale( "en","US" );
   df=DateFormat.getDateInstance( df.LONG, usa );
   out.print( "<li>USA date: "+ df.format( today ) );
%>
</ul>
</body> </html>
```

Locale specifies a language and a country using standard abbreviations – see page 112 for more info.

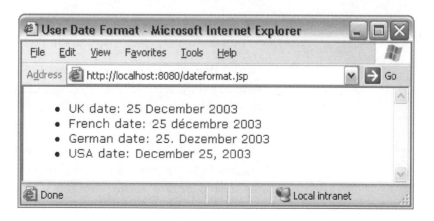

Formatting currency

Numbers, currency values and percentages are written in many different styles across the world. With currencies, some place their currency symbol before the amount, as in the UK, while others, like the French, prefer to place the symbol after the amount.

Web applications with JSP can format these values in a style that the user expects to see locally using the Java **NumberFormat** class. This works in a similar way to the **DateFormat** class that is used to format dates in the user's local style.

All the Java NumberFormat methods are made available to the page by importing the java.text package in a page directive. The java.util package is also imported to make the Locale class available.

The **NumberFormat** class has three methods called **getNumberInstance()**, used to format numbers only, **getPercentInstance()**, for formatting percentage numbers, and the **getCurrencyInstance()** that formats a number and adds the appropriate currency symbol in the expected position.

A user's location can first be discovered with the JSP **request.getLocale()** method, as described on page 112. This can then be specified as the argument to any of the **NumberFormat** methods to determine how they should format the number.

When the desired formatting has been specified the number can be translated into a String by the **NumberFormat.format()** method.

In this example the **request.getLocale()** method first assigns the user's locale to a **Locale** variable called **here**. A **NumberFormat** variable called **nf** is then assigned a currency instance which specifies that **Locale** as the required formatting style. The **NumberFormat.format()** method translates this into a String which is displayed in the output.

Further examples in the scriptlet set the **Locale** to other countries to show how the number appears in their local currency style.

Notice that European countries which use the Euro currency need to have a third argument specifying **EURO** when creating their new **Locale** object. This ensures that the Euro € symbol is displayed rather than that of their former currency.

It is also necessary to specify the **charset** character encoding in the **contentType** attribute of the page directive as one that can display the Euro € symbol. In this case it is set to **windows-1252**.

currency.jsp

```jsp
<%@ page language="java"
    contentType="text/html; charset=windows-1252" %>
<%@ page import="java.util.*, java.text.*" %>

<html><head> <title>User Currency Format</title> </head>
<body bgcolor="white"> <ul>

<% Locale here = request.getLocale();
   NumberFormat nf =
     NumberFormat.getCurrencyInstance(here);
   out.print( "<li>"+here.getDisplayCountry() +" - "
                                + nf.format(10000.00) );

   Locale france = new Locale("fr","FR","EURO");
   nf = NumberFormat.getCurrencyInstance(france);
   out.print( "<li>"+ france.getDisplayCountry() +" - "
                                + nf.format(10000.00) );

   Locale italy = new Locale("it","IT","EURO");
   nf = NumberFormat.getCurrencyInstance(italy);
   out.print( "<li>"+ italy.getDisplayCountry() +" - "
                                + nf.format(10000.00) );

   Locale usa = new Locale("en","US");
   nf = NumberFormat.getCurrencyInstance(usa);
   out.print( "<li>"+usa.getDisplayCountry() +" - "
                                + nf.format(10000.00) );
%>
</ul> </body> </html>
```

User Currency Format - Microsoft Internet Explorer

File   Edit   View   Favorites   Tools   Help

Address http://localhost:8080/currency.jsp   Go

- United Kingdom - £10,000.00
- France - 10 000,00 €
- Italy - € 10.000,00
- United States - $10,000.00

Done   Local intranet

Searching cookies

Cookies can offer a convenient way to store snippets of user-specific information in a file on the client computer. These may be accessed as required by the application and can be used to maintain data regarding the user's preferences or activities.

As the ability to write cookies can be disabled by the user in their browser options it is not a good idea to use cookies to maintain critical data though. Also, hand-held devices with Internet access may have insufficient features to allow the storage of cookie data. For these reasons an option should always be offered to the user where they may choose to allow cookies to be used, or not.

The JSP page cookiestart.jsp that processes this form and creates a cookie is detailed on page 120.

Cookies are only able to store information as String values. The maximum size of a cookie cannot exceed 4Kb and the total number of cookies cannot exceed 300. Information is stored in the cookie as a name/value pair which will remain accessible until the browser is closed, or until a pre-defined expiry time is reached.

The JSP page opposite looks for a previous cookie with the name of **username** by looping through all cookies returned by the **request.getCookies()** method to find a match. That cookie's value is then assigned to a String variable called **userValue**.

The value of the **userValue** variable is assigned to be the value of a form text input that will appear in the page shown below. Otherwise, this will be an empty string if no cookie is found. The submit button on this form takes the user to a second JSP page that will create a cookie if the user has checked this form's checkbox.

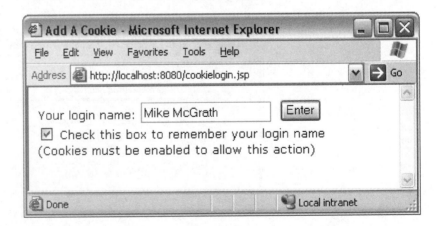

cookielogin.jsp

Submission passes form data as request parameters. These will be called 'username' and, if the checkbox has been checked, 'remember', together with their associated values.

```jsp
<%@ page language="java" contentType="text/html" %>
<%
// cookie name to seek
String myCookie = "username";

// declare a cookie value variable
String userValue = "";

// if any cookies are found...
if(request.getCookies() != null)
{
  // assign all cookies to an array...
  Cookie[] cookies = request.getCookies();

  // loop through the cookie array...
  for(int i=0; i<cookies.length; i++)
  {
    // if the current cookie name is that sought...
    if ( cookies[i].getName().equals( myCookie ) )
    {
      // assign it to the cookie value variable
      userValue = cookies[i].getValue();
    }
  }
}
%>

<html>
<head> <title>Add A Cookie</title> </head>
<body>

<form action="cookiestart.jsp" method="post">
  Your login name:
<input type="text" name="username"
       value="<%= userValue %>">
<input type="submit" value="Enter"><br/>
<input type="checkbox" name="remember" value="yes">
Check this box to remember your login name <br/>
(Cookies must be enabled to allow this action)
</form>
</body>
</html>
```

Creating cookies

The JSP page below processes the form shown on page 118 and creates a cookie when the user has checked the form's checkbox.

cookiestart.jsp

```
<%@ page language="java" contentType="text/html" %>
<%
String userValue = "";

if( request.getParameter("remember") != null )
{
  userValue = request.getParameter("username");

  // 1. create a new cookie to store the username
  Cookie myCookie = new Cookie("username", userValue);

  // 2. set cookie life to 1 hour (3600 seconds)
  myCookie.setMaxAge(3600);

  // 3. write the cookie
  response.addCookie( myCookie );
}
%>

<html> <head> <title>Start Page</title> </head>
<body>
Welcome <b> <%= userValue %> </b>!
</body>
</html>
```

The scriptlet first declares a String variable called **userValue** with a default empty string value. Then an **if** statement tests to see if the user has checked the checkbox, requesting to store the text input value, thus passing a request parameter named **remember**.

When the **remember** parameter is found, its value is assigned to the **userValue** variable for display on that page. Additionally a cookie called **username** is created to store the same value.

The life of the **username** cookie is set to one hour duration with the **Cookie.setMaxAge()** method and the cookie is finally written on the client system with the **response.addCookie()** method.

The displayed output is shown at the top of the opposite page.

...cont'd

The cookie cache on a Windows system is in the Temporary Internet Files directory.

The cookie is a simple text file that is placed in the cookie cache directory on the client system. Opening the cookie for this example reveals that the cookie contains the cookie name and value followed by the domain that created the cookie. This is the only domain that will be granted access to this cookie.

If the user returns to the **cookielogin.jsp** page (shown on page 118) during the life of this cookie, the stored value will automatically be read from the cookie and displayed in the text field:

Cookies or session data?

With JavaServer Pages, it is simpler, and more reliable, to store transient user information as **session** data rather than in cookies. This avoids the problems where a user has disabled cookies in the browser, or where the system does not support cookies, and requires less code.

The lines of code in the three steps that create a cookie in the example on page 120 can be replaced by this single line of code to store the same information as **session** data:

```
session.setAttribute("username", userValue);
```

This information can then be accessed at any point until the session is terminated, either explicitly or by closing the browser.

The following simple JSP page illustrates how another page opened during the same session can access the session data stored previously using the **session.getAttribute()** method:

sessionnext.jsp

```
<%@ page language="java" contentType="text/html" %>
<html> <head> <title>Session Next Page</title> </head>
<body>
Are you enjoying this session
<b><%= session.getAttribute("username") %></b>?
</body> </html>
```

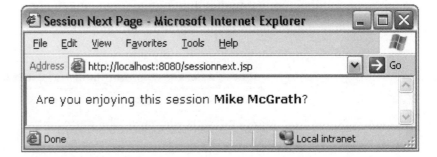

The ease of maintaining user information as session data makes this method preferable to using cookies for transient information such as shopping cart details. Cookies allow constant data, like login passwords, to be stored for longer periods that span sessions.

Creating JavaBeans

This chapter explains how to create JavaBeans for use with JavaServer Pages. It demonstrates both value-type beans, for data storage, and utility-type beans, for processing data. Additional information is provided on how commercial JavaBeans can be used in your JSP applications.

Covers

Chapter Ten

What is a JavaBean?

A JavaBean is a Java class that is written to comply with certain rules that are laid down in the JavaBean specifications. These enable a JavaBean to be regarded by a JSP developer as a facility in which they can store data or have data manipulated by simply passing the data to the JavaBean as an input parameter.

A JSP application may use original home-made JavaBeans, or commercial ready-made JavaBeans which require no knowledge of Java programming, or a mixture of both.

Java code within a JSP page can often be moved into a JavaBean to isolate an application's programming aspects. This cleans up the page code and simplifies its maintenance and development.

It is important to recognise that a JavaBean is a component that can be used by multiple JSP pages and applications. Several JavaBean components can be used to a build a single application to provide functionality such as database access or email messaging.

The rules for creating a JavaBean state that:

- The class must have an 'empty' constructor method – so it can be omitted entirely or just included to initialize variables

- Public variables are not allowed – only use private variables

- Variables names must start with a lowercase character

- Public accessor methods to a specific format should be included to assign and retrieve values stored in class variables

JavaBean variables are referred to as 'properties' in JSP pages.

- Accessor methods may only have a single argument

A JavaBean's accessors are known as **setter** and **getter** methods and are named using the name of the variable to which they apply. The variable name is changed to start with an uppercase character and is prefixed by either 'set' or 'get'. For instance, accessor methods for a variable called **name** would be **setName()** and **getName()**.

The return type of the **setter** method will always be **void,** because it does not return any value, whereas the return type of the **getter** method will match the type of the variable that it returns.

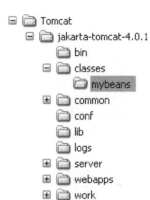

Tomcat
jakarta-tomcat-4.0.1
bin
classes
mybeans
common
conf
lib
logs
server
webapps
work

Typically JavaBeans are placed in a **package** that is the name of the folder in which they reside. For instance, all the JavaBean examples in this book are contained in a package folder called **mybeans**. This is situated in Tomcat's **classes** directory to ensure that the beans can be available to all applications. JavaBean source code is written in a **.java** file that begins with a **package** declaration specifying the name of its host folder.

The example below lists a JavaBean called **SimpleBean** that is located in the **mybeans** package folder. Like other Java programs the class name must exactly match the name of the file so this file is named **SimpleBean.java**.

SimpleBean.java

```
package mybeans;

public class SimpleBean
{
  // declare a variable (a bean property)
  private String message;

  // setter method assigns value to the message property
  public void setMessage(String input)
  {
    message = input;
  }

  // getter method returns value of the message property
  public String getMessage()
  {
    return message;
  }
}
```

See overleaf to discover how this example is compiled then used by JSP.

The **SimpleBean** class has just one variable which is a String type variable called **message**. A **setter** method called **setMessage()** specifies a single String argument that must be passed when the method is called. The value of the argument is then assigned to the **message** variable by this **setter** method. The value stored inside the **message** variable will be returned when the **getter** method named **getMessage()** is called. No constructor method is included.

Compiling JavaBeans

Before a JavaBean can be used with JavaServer Pages its **.java** file must be compiled to create a **.class** file. This can be achieved with the **javac** compiler tool that was introduced in the Java crash course chapter earlier in this book.

To compile the **SimpleBean.java** example from the previous page a command prompt needs to be opened in its host folder then the command **javac SimpleBean.java** entered at the prompt.

At a command prompt type javac -help to see a list of all available compiler options.

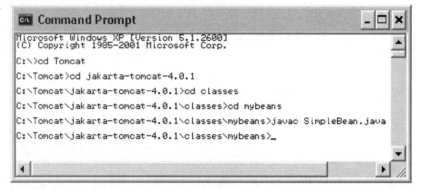

When the **enter** key is pressed the command is executed and the **javac** compiler begins the compilation process. Upon completion, focus returns to the command line and a **.class file** bearing the same file name is added to the host folder alongside the **.java** source file. The SimpleBean JavaBean is now ready for use in a JSP page, as is demonstrated on the facing page.

Utilising JavaBeans

To use the SimpleBean JavaBean from the opposite page an instance of that bean's class must first be created on the JSP page with a **useBean** action element. Values can then be assigned to its variable with the **setProperty** action element and retrieved from it with the **getProperty** action element:

simplebean.jsp

For more on the useBean action element refer back to page 32. Also see page 34 for more on the setProperty and getProperty action elements.

```
<%@ page language="java" contentType="text/html" %>
<html><head><title>Using SimpleBean</title></head><body>

<%-- create an instance of the SimpleBean JavaBean
     and give it the id name of 'msg' --%>
<jsp:useBean id="msg" class="mybeans.SimpleBean" />

<%-- call the bean instance's setter method to
     assign a value to its 'message' variable --%>
<jsp:setProperty name="msg"
     property="message" value="Saying Hello" />

<%-- call the bean instance's getter method to retrieve
     the value stored in its 'message' variable --%>
<jsp:getProperty name="msg" property="message" />

<%-- call the bean instance's setter method to assign a
     new value to its 'message' variable --%>
<jsp:setProperty name="msg" property="message"
                             value=" with a JavaBean" />

<%-- call the bean instance's getter method to retrieve
     the new value stored in its 'message' variable --%>
<jsp:getProperty name="msg" property="message" />

</body> </html>
```

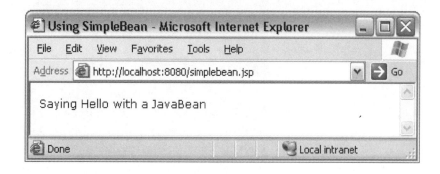

Setting all properties at once

For those JavaBeans that store information from a submitted HTML form, JavaServer Pages offers a special technique that can be used to set all the bean's variable values at once.

To use this technique it is essential that the names of the bean's variables are identical to the names of the form's input fields.

This is a short-cut that avoids setting the properties individually.

The JSP page specified by the form's **action** attribute can create an instance of the storage bean with a **useBean** element in the usual way. It can then set all its variables by assigning a ★ wildcard character to the property attribute of a **setProperty** action element. So the syntax to set all the bean's variables looks like this:

```
<jsp:useBean id= "instanceName" class= "beanName" />
<jsp:setProperty name= "instanceName" property= "★" />
```

The following example starts from a HTML page called **valuebean.html** that contains a simple form housing three input fields called **name**, **city** and **colour**. The form's **action** attribute specifies that a JSP page called **valuebean.jsp** will handle the form data when the form is submitted to the server. The data will be assigned to variables in a JavaBean called **ValueBean** that is located in a package called **mybeans** within Tomcat's **classes** folder.

valuebean.html

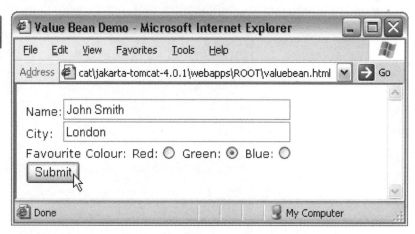

The source code of the **ValueBean** and the JSP page is shown opposite. After storing the data in instance variables of this bean the JSP page retrieves each value for display in a generated list.

ValueBean.java

Remember that the .java file must be compiled before the bean can be used in this example.

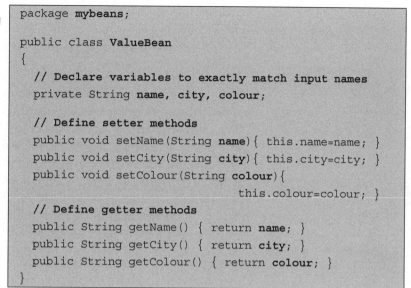

```java
package mybeans;

public class ValueBean
{
    // Declare variables to exactly match input names
    private String name, city, colour;

    // Define setter methods
    public void setName(String name){ this.name=name; }
    public void setCity(String city){ this.city=city; }
    public void setColour(String colour){
                                    this.colour=colour; }
    // Define getter methods
    public String getName() { return name; }
    public String getCity() { return city; }
    public String getColour() { return colour; }
}
```

valuebean.jsp

```jsp
<%@ page language="java" contentType="text/html" %>
<html> <head><title>Value Bean Demo</title> </head>
<body>
<jsp:useBean id="box" class="mybeans.ValueBean" />
<jsp:setProperty name="box" property="*" />
<ul>
<li>Name: <jsp:getProperty name="box" property="name" />
<li>City: <jsp:getProperty name="box" property="city" />
<li>Favourite Colour:
        <jsp:getProperty name="box" property="colour" />

</ul> </body> </html>
```

JavaBeans that do more

In addition to storing values as properties, JavaBeans can provide functionality by performing manipulation of property values. This naturally creates many more possibilities and greatly enhances the usefulness of JavaBeans.

The following example JavaBean demonstrates added functionality by calculating a range of property values from just one given value. It has a single **setter** method so that a JSP **setProperty** action element can assign a value to a variable called **cost**. This value represents the cost price of an item and is used by the **setter** method to perform a range of calculations. The result of each calculation is assigned to other variables that represent a 20% markup on the original cost, a subtotal of cost and markup, a VAT component of 17½%, and a grand overall total.

A **getter** method allows retrieval of the original **cost** property and other **getter** methods allow individual retrieval of all the properties formatted as UK currency values.

bean2.java

```
package mybeans ;

public class bean2
{
  /* DECLARE VARIABLES (PROPERTIES) */

  double cost;
  double markup;
  double subtotal;
  double vat;
  double total;


  /* THE SETTER METHOD */

  public void setCost(double cost)
  {
    this.cost = cost;
    this.markup= ( (cost / 100) * 20 );
    this.subtotal= (cost + markup );
    this.vat=( (subtotal / 100) * 17.5 );
    this.total=( subtotal + vat );
  }
}
```

*bean2.java
(continued)*

```java
/* THE GETTER METHODS */

public double getCost() { return cost; }

public String getCostPrice(){ return doFormat(cost); }

public String getMarkup(){ return doFormat(markup); }

public String getSubtotal(){
                        return doFormat(subtotal); }

public String getVat() { return doFormat(vat); }

public String getTotal() { return doFormat(total); }


/* CURRENCY FORMATTING UTILITY METHOD */

private String doFormat(double sum)
{
  java.util.Locale loc =
                    new java.util.Locale("en","GB");
  java.text.NumberFormat nf =
      java.text.NumberFormat.getCurrencyInstance(loc);
  return nf.format(sum);
}
}
```

For more on formatting refer to the last chapter and see page 116.

Setting the **cost** property to a value of **10.00** creates the property values shown across the HTML table illustrated below:

The JSP that generates this output using the bean2 JavaBean is fully listed on page 35.

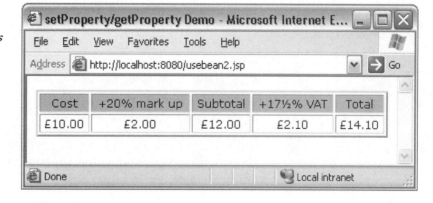

Cost	+20% mark up	Subtotal	+17½% VAT	Total
£10.00	£2.00	£12.00	£2.10	£14.10

Ready-made JavaBeans

One big advantage of developing component-based applications is that ready-made third-party components can be adopted for your own purposes. This is especially true of JavaBean components which can be used to develop new JSP applications – the JSP developer need only know a bean's property names and methods to include it in an application.

JavaBean components can be found on the Internet, for sale or free download, at a number of locations. Utilising these resources can reduce development time so a project can be completed quickly. It can, therefore, be worthwhile to look for ready-made JavaBeans for your required needs before starting to produce your own code.

A good starting point when looking for ready-made JavaBeans is the JavaBeans Listings page on the Java Applet Rating Service (JARS) website at `www.jars.com/jars_resources_javabeans.html`. The JavaBean components here are given ratings to indicate how successfully they fulfil their intended purpose.

IBM also offers a number of JavaBean components for free download at their AlphaWorks website which can be found at `www.alphaworks.ibm.com/alphaBeans`. These are well documented and worth exploring.

Another source of ready-made JavaBeans is the ScriptSearch website at `www.scriptsearch.com`. You will find the JavaBeans here classified under **JSP and Servlets** in the Java archive.

Commercial JavaBeans covering almost every conceivable topic are available for purchase from the Component Resource website at `www.componentsource.com`. This site boasts, with some justification, that it is the definitive source of software components. While some of the offerings may seem a little pricey, commercial JavaBean components will have been rigorously tested and should, therefore, provide assured performance reliability.

Whatever source is used, it may be possible to build your entire complex JSP application with ready-made JavaBeans, and without writing a single line of Java code.

Custom JSP actions

This chapter describes how to create custom JSP action elements which can be reused to perform common tasks. These custom element tags are simple to use and can be grouped into a Tag Library for implementation by anyone with a basic knowledge of HTML. Examples demonstrate how to build and deploy three different custom actions.

Covers

Chapter Eleven

What is a custom tag?

Custom JSP tags look similar to regular HTML elements but can dynamically insert content or functionality into a page as it is being processed. The precise nature of the task that it performs is specified in a Java class which defines that particular tag.

Custom tags provide a simpler alternative to JavaBeans for the JSP page author and offer an excellent way to separate logic from content. A whole range of custom tags can be grouped into a **tag library** to produce a powerful arsenal of functionality and formatting ability.

Typically, a tag library is created by a programmer so that functionality can be easily incorporated into a JSP page by anyone with just basic knowledge of HTML.

You do not need to know XML – a complete example of a Tag Library Descriptor file is given on page 136.

These three components are essential to deploy a custom tag:

- A Java tag handler class that implements the tag's functionality.

- A Tag Library Descriptor (TLD) in the form of a XML file describing the tag – typically located in the **WEB-INF** folder.

- A JSP page that includes the custom tag within a page.

The tag handler class that defines the action must have access to subclasses of the Java **javax.servlet.jsp.tagext** class. These contain methods and properties to create custom action tags.

The **javax.servlet.jsp.tagext** class can be found in the Enterprise Edition of the Java Development Kit (version 1.3.1) within the **lib/j2ee.jar** file, and also in the **lib/servlet.jar** file in the Java Web Services Developer Pack. Both can be freely downloaded from the Sun website at http://java.sun.com.

To make the classes available when compiling tag handler classes the **javax/servlet/jsp/tagext** directory structure can be extracted from the jar file and simply copied into the folder containing the tag handler classes.

With the required Java classes in place the three ingredients listed above can be added to create a custom action tag. Several custom action tags are created in the examples in this chapter.

Creating a tag handler class

The first ingredient required to produce custom action elements is the Java code that will implement the tags' action. These can conveniently be located in Tomcat's **classes** directory in a folder called **mytags** so that they will be available to any JSP application.

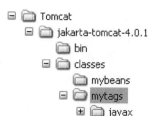

The simplest example to start with is a tag with no attributes that will just insert content into the body of a generated page. The code listed below begins by declaring itself to be part of the **mytags** package then imports the required Java classes.

HelloTag.java/HelloTag.class

```java
package mytags;

import javax.servlet.jsp.*;
import javax.servlet.jsp.tagext.*;
import java.io.*;

public class HelloTag extends TagSupport
{
  public int doStartTag()
  {
    try { JspWriter out = pageContext.getOut();
          out.print("Hello from CustomTag!"); }
    catch(IOException err)
      { System.out.print("Error: "+err); }
    return(SKIP_BODY);
  }
}
```

This file should be located in Tomcat in a classes/mytags folder and compiled – see overleaf for the other ingredients needed with this example.

Notice that the class declaration extends the Java **TagSupport** class that contains methods and properties which are needed to form custom tag actions. The **doStartTag()** method is called when the custom tag is encountered and returns an integer denoting how to treat the body of the tag. In this case the **SKIP_BODY** constant specifies that the body should be ignored.

The tag handler must be compiled into a .class file before it can be used in a JSP page.

The **try-catch** statement block attempts to obtain the **JSPWriter** object from the **pageContext** so it can write a message on the page. If this fails an error message will be written instead.

Creating a Tag Library Descriptor

A Tag Library Descriptor is a simple XML file normally located in the **WEB-INF** folder. The TLD listed below contains a description for the custom tag example on the previous page.

The TLD starts, like all XML files, with a standard XML declaration giving the version number. This is followed by a **DOCTYPE** declaration for the **taglib** XML element.

mytags.tld

```
<?xml version="1.0" ?>

<!DOCTYPE taglib PUBLIC
"-//Sun Microsystems, Inc.//DTD JSP Tag Library 1.2//EN"
"http://java.sun.com/j2ee/dtd/web-
jsptaglibrary_1_2.dtd">

<taglib>
  <tlib-version>1.0</tlib-version>
  <jsp-version>1.2</jsp-version>
  <short-name>mytagslib</short-name>
  <description>My Custom Tags Library</description>

  <tag>
    <name>hello</name>
    <tag-class>mytags.HelloTag</tag-class>
    <body-content>empty</body-content>
    <description>Display a greeting</description>
  </tag>
</taglib>
```

More tags can be added to this library by adding further <tag> </tag> element definition blocks.

The **taglib** element tags contain other nested elements that describe the library and each custom tag that it contains. In the example above the library version and JSP version are specified together with a name and description of this library.

The **tag** element tags contain other nested tags that define a custom JSP tag. This example describes a single tag called **hello** whose custom action is implemented by the Java **HelloTag** class located in the **mytags** package. If the action does not affect the body of the custom tag it is important to specify **empty** in the **body-content** element.

Using a custom action tag

Having created a tag handler class and included the tag's description in the Tag Library Descriptor file means that the custom tag is ready for use in JSP pages.

The tag is first made available to a JSP page by defining the location of the TLD file in a **taglib** directive element. The address is assigned to a **uri** attribute of this element and its **prefix** attribute must be assigned a short prefix to proceed the tag name when it is used on the page.

The simple JSP page shown below states the location of the **mytags.tld** file listed on the facing page and specifies that the prefix **mytag** should proceed the tag name on this page.

The custom tag named as **hello** in the TLD can now feature in this page by including the element <mytag:hello />.

hellotag.jsp

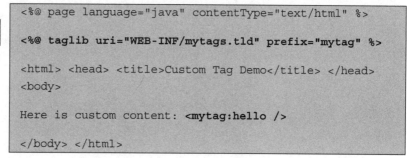

```
<%@ page language="java" contentType="text/html" %>

<%@ taglib uri="WEB-INF/mytags.tld" prefix="mytag" %>

<html> <head> <title>Custom Tag Demo</title> </head>
<body>

Here is custom content: <mytag:hello />

</body> </html>
```

HOT TIP

*The final /
character
inside the tag
denotes that
this is an
empty tag that has no
body content.*

When the page is processed the text content is written by the Java **HelloTag** class into the generated output shown below:

A custom tag to display the date

Besides inserting text into a page, custom action tags can call on the power of the Java classes to provide even more functionality.

A simple way to demonstrate this principle features the **java.util.Date** class that can be used to create a **Date** object containing information about the date and time of its creation.

In the following example a tag handler class called **DateTag** creates a **Date** object named **today** that can be written out in a JSP page by a custom action tag. The **DateTag.java** file listed below is placed in the **mytags** folder, as described on page 135, then compiled to create a **DateTag.class** file.

DateTag.java / DateTag.class

This code is similar to the previous example on page 135 but now creates a Date object that is written on the page.

```
package mytags;

import javax.servlet.jsp.*;
import javax.servlet.jsp.tagext.*;
import java.io.*;

public class DateTag extends TagSupport
{
  java.util.Date today = new java.util.Date();

  public int doStartTag()
  {
    try
    {
      JspWriter out = pageContext.getOut();
      out.print(today);
    }
    catch(IOException err)
    {
      System.out.print("Error: "+err);
    }
    return(SKIP_BODY);
  }
}
```

The description of the custom tag using the **DateTag** class can now be added to the Tag Library Descriptor **mytags.tld**, introduced on page 136, by inserting the following **<tag>** element block inside the **<taglib>** element tags:

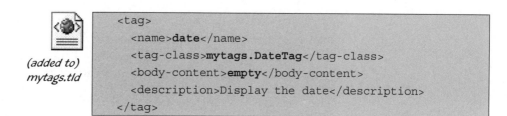

(added to)
mytags.tld

```
<tag>
  <name>date</name>
  <tag-class>mytags.DateTag</tag-class>
  <body-content>empty</body-content>
  <description>Display the date</description>
</tag>
```

This addition to the TLD describes a tag named **date** that employs the **DateTag** class located within the **mytags** folder in Tomcat's **classes** directory. The tag will never have any body content so is defined as an **empty** tag.

The **date** custom action tag can now be used in a JSP page by declaring the location of the TLD with a **taglib** directive.

The simple JSP page shown below sets the custom tag prefix as **mytag** so the date at which the page is processed can be written on the generated page using **<mytag:date />**.

datetag.jsp

```
<%@ page language="java" contentType="text/html" %>

<%@ taglib uri="WEB-INF/mytags.tld" prefix="mytag" %>

<html> <head> <title>Custom Tag Demo</title> </head>
<body>

Today's date is: <mytag:date />

</body> </html>
```

The output page generated by the code above looks like this:

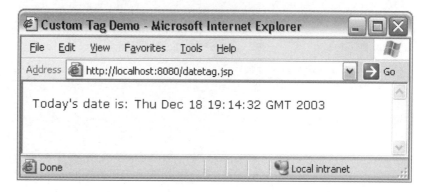

Adding attributes to a custom tag

Attributes can be added to custom tags so that the page author can include specifications when using the tag. This example builds on the example on the previous page to create a custom tag that will write the date in a format specified in an attribute.

The Java class listed below has a setter method that assigns the specified attribute value to a variable called **style**. This is tested by an **if-else** block in the **doStartTag()** method for values of **short**, **medium** or **long**. The date is then written on the page in the format specified by the **style** variable.

FormattedDateTag.java / FormattedDateTag.class

The only permissible values in this example are short, medium and long – anything else will cause an error.

```
package mytags;
import javax.servlet.jsp.*;
import javax.servlet.jsp.tagext.*;
import java.io.*;  import java.text.*;

public class FormattedDateTag extends TagSupport
{
  java.util.Date today = new java.util.Date();
  DateFormat date;
  private String style;

  public void setStyle(String specified)
  { style = specified; }

  public int doStartTag()
  { try
    { JspWriter out = pageContext.getOut();
    if (style.equals("short"))
    date= DateFormat.getDateInstance(DateFormat.SHORT);
    else if (style.equals("medium"))
    date=DateFormat.getDateInstance(DateFormat.MEDIUM);
    else if (style.equals("long"))
    date = DateFormat.getDateInstance(DateFormat.LONG);
    out.print( date.format(today) );
    }
    catch(IOException err)
    { System.out.println("Error: " + err); }
  return(SKIP_BODY);
  }
}
```

…cont'd

The Java class shown opposite can be added to the TLD by including the tag description shown below. This creates a custom tag named **fdate** with an optional attribute called **style**. JSP code is allowed to be assigned to this attribute by the inclusion of the **rtexprvalue** element with a **true** value.

added to mytags.tld – see page 136.

```
<tag>
  <name>fdate</name>
  <tag-class>mytags.FormattedDateTag</tag-class>
  <body-content>empty</body-content>
  <attribute>
    <name>style</name>
    <required>false</required>
    <rtexprvalue>true</rtexprvalue>
  </attribute>
</tag>
```

The following simple JSP page writes the date in each of the three possible formats by assigning the permissible values to the **style** attribute of the **fdate** custom tag.

formatteddatetag.jsp

```
<%@ page language="java" contentType="text/html" %>
<%@ taglib uri="/WEB-INF/mytags.tld" prefix="mytag" %>

<html> <head><title>Custom Tag Demo</title> </head>
<body> Short Date:<mytag:fdate style="short" /> <br/>
       Medium Date:<mytag:fdate style="medium" /> <br/>
       Long Date:<mytag:fdate style="long" />
</body> </html>
```

For more on date formatting see page 114.

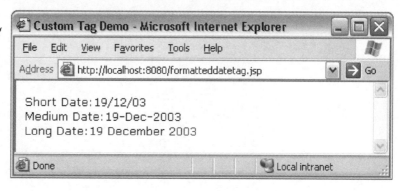

Short Date: 19/12/03
Medium Date: 19-Dec-2003
Long Date: 19 December 2003

Formatting the custom tag body

A pair of custom tags can enclose content so that it can be formatted by a Java tag handler class. When this type of custom tag is encountered on a page the tag handler's **doStartTag()** method can write HTML formatting code on the page. This method returns a constant called **EVAL_BODY_INCLUDE** to ensure that the tag's body content is also written on the page.

When the custom closing tag is encountered the tag handler's **doEndTag()** method can write the closing HTML code. This method returns a constant called **EVAL_PAGE** to ensure that the rest of the page is processed.

The following example demonstrates how a custom tag called **block** is used to format some of the page content:

BlockTag.java/BlockTag.class

```
package mytags;
import javax.servlet.jsp.*;
import javax.servlet.jsp.tagext.*; import java.io.*;

public class BlockTag extends TagSupport
{
  public int doStartTag()
  { try
    { JspWriter out = pageContext.getOut();
      out.print("<div style='border:ridge 12px #C0C0C0;
        padding:5px; width:75%; font-weight:bold'>");
    }
    catch(IOException err)
      { System.out.println("Error: " + err); }
    return(EVAL_BODY_INCLUDE);
  }

  public int doEndTag()
  { try
    { JspWriter out = pageContext.getOut();
      out.print("</div>");
    }
    catch(IOException err)
      { System.out.println("Error: " + err); }
    return(EVAL_PAGE);
  }
}
```

The Java class shown opposite can be placed in the **mytags** folder of Tomcat's **classes** directory and compiled. The tag description shown below can be added to the TLD **mytags.tld** started on page 136 to create the custom tag named **block**. It is important to note that the **body-content** element must now enclose the term **JSP** to be effective.

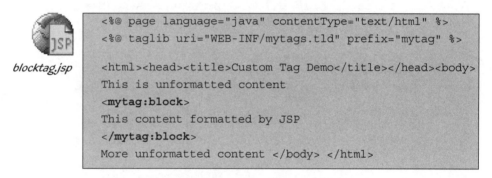

(added to) mytags.tld

```
<tag>
  <name>block</name>
  <tag-class>mytags.BlockTag</tag-class>
  <body-content>JSP</body-content>
</tag>
```

The simple JSP page listed below illustrates how the **block** custom tag formats the appearance of its enclosed content by making the text bold and surrounding it with a ridge border.

blocktag.jsp

```
<%@ page language="java" contentType="text/html" %>
<%@ taglib uri="WEB-INF/mytags.tld" prefix="mytag" %>

<html><head><title>Custom Tag Demo</title></head><body>
This is unformatted content
<mytag:block>
This content formatted by JSP
</mytag:block>
More unformatted content </body> </html>
```

Modifying the custom tag body

In the example on the previous page the formatting was carried out by the extra HTML instructions that the custom tag wrote on the page. The body content of a custom tag can itself be modified by the tag handler class and then written on the page.

To achieve this the tag handler class must extend the **BodyTagSupport** class, rather than the **TagSupport** class that has been extended in all this chapter's previous examples. This is used in the following example to modify all the body content of the custom tag to uppercase characters.

This tag handler class has a single **doAfterBody()** method that initially assigns the custom tag's body content to a **BodyContent** object named **body**. The **getString()** method of this object then assigns the tag's body content to a String variable called **text**. This is finally written out in modified form by appending the **toUpperCase()** method. Notice that the return value is set to **SKIP_BODY** so that the original content of the custom tag is ignored when the processing continues.

*CapitalTag.java /
CapitalTag.class*

```
package mytags;
import javax.servlet.jsp.*;
import javax.servlet.jsp.tagext.*;
import java.io.*;

public class CapitalTag extends BodyTagSupport
{
  public int doAfterBody()
  {
    BodyContent body = getBodyContent();
    String text = body.getString();
    try
    {
      JspWriter out = body.getEnclosingWriter();
      out.print( text.toUpperCase() );
    }
    catch(IOException err)
    { System.out.println("Error: " + err); }
    return(SKIP_BODY);
  }
}
```

The **CapitalTag** class can be placed in the **mytags** folder of Tomcat's **classes** directory and compiled. The following tag description can then be added to the TLD **mytags.tld**, started on page 136, to create a custom tag named **caps**.

(added to)
mytags.tld

```
<tag>
  <name>caps</name>
  <tag-class>mytags.CapitalTag</tag-class>
  <body-content>JSP</body-content>
</tag>
```

The simple JSP page listed below illustrates how the **caps** custom tag formats the appearance of its enclosed content by writing an uppercase version of the content onto the page.

capitaltag.jsp

```
<%@ page language="java" contentType="text/html" %>

<%@ taglib uri="WEB-INF/mytags.tld" prefix="mytag" %>

<html> <head><title>Custom Tag Demo</title> </head>
<body>

<p>This is unformatted content</p>

<mytag:caps>This content formatted by Java</mytag:caps>

<p>More unformatted content</p>
</body> </html>
```

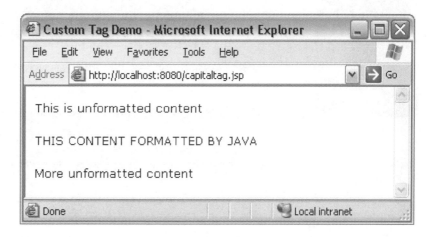

Using existing tag libraries

There may be no need to build your own custom tags as there are ready-made tag libraries available for free on the Internet. It is always worth checking to see if the functionality you want to produce can be achieved using ready-made tags in a free library.

There are existing custom tags to send email messages, access databases, produce graphs and charts, build tables, draw graphics, transform XML and almost anything else you can think of.

These three great websites offer tag libraries for free download and are well worth exploring:

The Jakarta Project: http://jakarata.apache.org/taglibs

JSPtags.com: http://jsptags.com/tags

JSP Resource Index: http://www.jspin.com

For more on WML and WMLScript please refer to 'WAP in easy steps':

There are also JSP tag libraries for download from ColdJava at `http://coldjava.hypermart.net` including one for WAP developers that handles WML element tags at `http://coldjava.hypermart.net/servlets/wmltags.htm`.

MySQL databases

This chapter illustrates how to store information in a database. It details how to install the free MySQL database server and demonstrates some basics of the Structured Query Language (SQL) that is used to add and manipulate data in a database.

Covers

Chapter Twelve

Introducing databases

Databases are simply convenient storage containers that store data in a structured manner. Every database is composed of one or more tables that structure the data into organized rows and columns. This makes it easier to reference and manipulate the data.

Each database table column has a label to identify the data stored within the table cells in that column. Each row contains an entry called a **record** that places data in each cell along that row.

A typical simple database table looks like this:

```
+-----------+-------+---------+----------+----------------+
| member_id | fname | lname   | tel      | email          |
+-----------+-------+---------+----------+----------------+
|         1 | John  | Smith   | 555-1234 | john@mail.com  |
|         2 | Anne  | Jones   | 555-5678 | anne@mail.com  |
|         3 | Mike  | McGrath | 555-3456 | mike@mail.com  |
+-----------+-------+---------+----------+----------------+
```

The column labels feature an underscore character because spaces are not allowed in labels.

The rows of a database table are not automatically arranged in any particular order so they can be sorted alphabetically, numerically or by any other criteria. It is important, therefore, to have some means to identify each record in the table. The example above allocates a **member id** for this purpose and this unique identifier is known as the **primary key**.

Storing data in a single table is very useful but **relational** databases with multiple tables introduce more possibilities by allowing the stored data to be combined in a variety of ways. For instance, the following two tables could be added to the database containing the first example table shown above:

```
+----------+-------------+          +-----------+----------+
| video_id | title       |          | member_id | video_id |
+----------+-------------+          +-----------+----------+
|        1 | Titanic     |          |         2 |        1 |
|        2 | Men In Black|          |         1 |        3 |
|        3 | Star Wars   |          |         3 |        2 |
+----------+-------------+          +-----------+----------+
```

The second table lists several video titles sorted numerically by **video id** number. The third table describes a relationship between the first and second table that links each member to the video they have rented. So Anne (member #2) has Titanic (video #1), John (member #1) has Star Wars (video #3) and Mike (member #3) has Men In Black (video #2).

Installing MySQL

There are a variety of database servers available for purchase, such as Microsoft Access, but the MySQL database server is both powerful and free. It is in widespread use on Web servers running JavaServer Pages and can be freely downloaded from www.mysql.com. Microsoft Access is not suitable for many Web databases so MySQL is used in all examples in this book.

MySQL is available for Windows and Unix/Linux platforms. Choose the latest binary release version of MySQL for Windows from the website and download it in a single zip file containing the **setup.exe** installer. Run setup and choose a convenient location for the installation, such as **C:\MySQL**. The installation includes a folder named **Docs** containing helpful guidance in a file called **manual.html**.

Before the MySQL database server can be started the configuration file **C:\MySQL\my-example.cnf** must be copied to the root directory at **C:** and renamed to **mycnf.cnf**. The options set in this file are read by MySQL whenever it is started.

The **C:\MySQL\bin** folder contains all the executable files to run MySQL. On Windows XP, 2000 and NT systems MySQL can be installed as a service that runs in the background but other platforms have to run MySQL manually as an application.

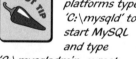
On Windows 9x platforms type 'C:\mysqld' to start MySQL and type 'C:\mysqladmin -u root shutdown' to stop MySQL.

Type **C:\mysql\bin\mysqld-nt --install** at a command prompt to install the MySQL service. The service can then be started from a prompt with the command **NET START mysql** or stopped with **NET STOP mysql**. With MySQL running type **C:\MySQL\bin\mysql** to open the MySQL monitor where databases can be created and manipulated:

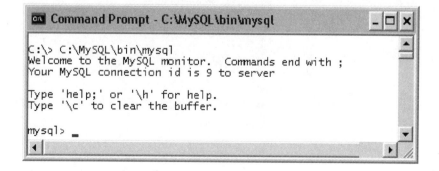

Creating a new database

MySQL databases can be created and their contents amended or queried in the MySQL monitor using instructions in the Structured Query Language (SQL).

In Windows XP the MySQL server can be started, paused and stopped by the Management Console in Control Panel > Administrative Tools > Services.

Ensure that the MySQL server is running (see previous page) then at a prompt type the command **C:\MySQL\bin\mysql** to open the MySQL monitor. The response acknowledges that the monitor is now open and the command prompt changes to **mysql>** awaiting input of some SQL instruction.

The SQL command to create a new database is, unsurprisingly, **create database** followed by your choice of name for the new database. MySQL is not case sensitive but each SQL command must be terminated with a semi-colon. So the complete command of **create database garage;** creates a new database called 'garage'.

The MySQL monitor responds by confirming that the new database has been created with the message **Query OK** followed by information about affected rows and time elapsed.

The names of all databases on the MySQL server can be viewed with the SQL **show databases** command to confirm that the new 'garage' database does indeed exist:

If you would prefer to avoid working with MySQL from a prompt try one of the free GUI front ends, such as the excellent MySQL-Front at www. mysqlfront.de.

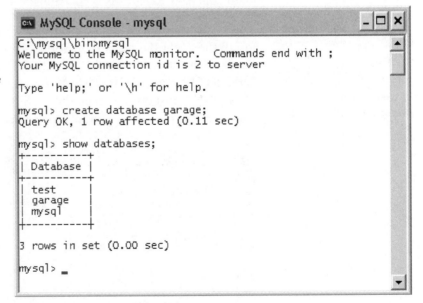

```
MySQL Console - mysql

C:\mysql\bin>mysql
Welcome to the MySQL monitor.  Commands end with ;
Your MySQL connection id is 2 to server

Type 'help;' or '\h' for help.

mysql> create database garage;
Query OK, 1 row affected (0.11 sec)

mysql> show databases;
+----------+
| Database |
+----------+
| test     |
| garage   |
| mysql    |
+----------+
3 rows in set (0.00 sec)

mysql>
```

Creating a database table

Before creating a database table you must first select the database where it is to be added using the SQL **use** command. This is followed by the name of one of the existing databases, revealed by the **show databases** command.

Remember that a semi-colon is required after each complete command.

A new table is created with the SQL **create table** command followed by a chosen name for that table, then a comma-separated list of chosen column names enclosed within a pair of brackets. Additionally each column name must be followed by a data type specifier to determine the type of data permitted in the table cells of that column. Typically these specifiers can state the SQL keywords of **int** for integer numbers, **decimal** for floating-point numbers, or **text** for character strings.

For instance, the syntax to create a database table with three columns is **create table** *tablename (column1-name column1-type, column2-name column2-type, column3-name column3-type);*

Once a database has been selected the SQL **show tables** command reveals the name of all tables in that database. This is used in the MySQL monitor illustrated below to confirm the addition of a table called 'cars' to the 'garage' database created on the facing page. The 'cars' table contains one numeric column called 'id', and two text columns called 'make' and 'model'. Other SQL column types and further table creation options are described overleaf.

To close the MySQL monitor type 'exit' or 'quit' at the MySQL prompt.

```
MySQL Console - mysql                           _ □ ✕

mysql> use garage;
Database changed
mysql> create table cars(id int,make text,model text);
Query OK, 0 rows affected (0.00 sec)

mysql> show tables;
+----------------+
| Tables_in_garage |
+----------------+
| cars             |
+----------------+
1 row in set (0.00 sec)

mysql> _
```

SQL data types

The table below describes the range of data type specifiers that can be used when creating table columns in MySQL. It is advisable to specify the permitted data type precisely. For instance, if a column is only going to hold short strings use **varchar()** rather than **text**.

An enum type can contain up to 65535 permissible elements.

Type	Description
int	An integer from -2147483648 to 2147483647
decimal	A floating point number that can specify the number of permissible digits. For example decimal(3,2) allows -999.99 to 999.99
double	A long double-precision floating point number
date	A date in the YYY-MM-DD format
time	A time in the HH:MM:SS format
datetime	A combined date and time in the format YYYY-MM-DD HH:MM:SS
year	A year 1901-2155 in either YY or YYYY format
timestamp	Automatic date and time of last record entry
char()	A string of defined <u>fixed</u> length up to 255 characters long. For example, char(100) pads a smaller string to make it 100 characters long
varchar()	A string of defined <u>variable</u> length up to 255 characters long that is stored without padding
text	A string up to 65535 characters long
blob	A binary type for variable data
enum	A single string value from a defined list. For example, enum("red","green","blue") allows entry of any one of these three colours only
set	A string or multiple strings from a defined list. For example, set("red","green","blue") allows entry of one or more of these three colours

SQL field modifiers

In addition to specifying permissible data types when creating database table columns the modifiers described in the following table can optionally be stated to further control how a column should be used:

Modifier	Description
not null	Insists that each record must include data entry in this column
unique	Insists that records may not duplicate any entry in this column
auto_increment	Available only for numeric columns to automatically generate a number that is one more than the previous value in that column
primary key()	Specifies as its argument the name of the column to be used as the primary key for that table. For example, primary key(id)

Modifiers could be included when creating the 'cars' table on page 151 to produce a table with better defined columns. The **create table** command shown in the MySQL monitor below can automatically number the primary key **id** column. Each record must now include data in the **make** and **model** columns although no duplicate entries are permitted in the **model** column.

At the MySQL prompt type 'explain cars;' to see how the table is defined.

```
mysql> use garage;
Database changed
mysql> create table cars(id int auto_increment,
                         make varchar(20) not null,
                         model varchar(20) not null unique,
                         primary key(id) );
Query OK, 0 rows affected (0.00 sec)

mysql>
```

Inserting table data

Once a table has been created in a MySQL database, data can be entered into it with the SQL **insert into** command.
The syntax to enter a complete record across a row is:
insert into *tablename* **values(** *value1, value2, value3* **);**

The data values are entered as comma-separated arguments to the SQL **values()** function and the list must correspond to the number of table columns and, of course, each must be of the correct type.

Remember to enclose string data inside quotes when inserting data.

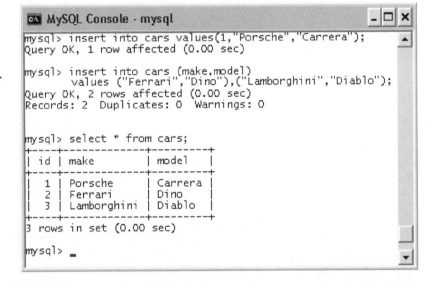

Another way to insert data into a table is to specify the column names where the data is to be added as a comma-separated list inside brackets after the table name in an **insert into** command. The actual data to be inserted into the specified columns is then listed as the **values()** function arguments as usual.

SQL instructions in the illustration use both methods to add three records to the 'cars' table created on the previous page. Notice that the **id** value for the second and third records has been generated automatically because of that column's **auto_increment** modifier.

An entire table can be viewed with a SQL **select ★ from** command, followed by the name of the table, and the obligatory semi-colon. The example above uses this command to view the 'cars' table.

Altering an existing table

The definition of a column in an existing table can be altered using the SQL commands **alter table** and **modify**, with the following syntax:

alter table *tablename* **modify** *fieldname type modifiers* ;

New columns can be added to an existing table using the same **alter table** command but now with the SQL **add** keyword. The syntax to add an extra column looks like this:

alter table *tablename* **add** *fieldname type modifiers* ;

The example shown in the MySQL monitor below uses the **alter table** command to add a new extra column to the 'cars' table from the previous page:

The new top_mph column does not have a 'not null' modifier so it is optional to enter data here.

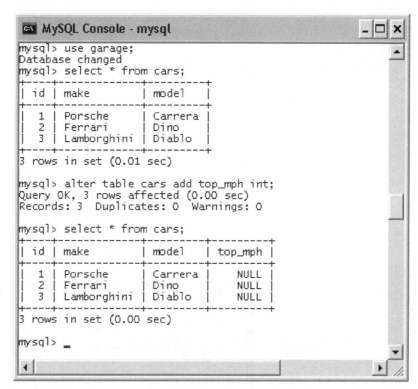

```
mysql> use garage;
Database changed
mysql> select * from cars;
+----+-------------+--------+
| id | make        | model  |
+----+-------------+--------+
|  1 | Porsche     | Carrera|
|  2 | Ferrari     | Dino   |
|  3 | Lamborghini | Diablo |
+----+-------------+--------+
3 rows in set (0.01 sec)

mysql> alter table cars add top_mph int;
Query OK, 3 rows affected (0.00 sec)
Records: 3  Duplicates: 0  Warnings: 0

mysql> select * from cars;
+----+-------------+--------+---------+
| id | make        | model  | top_mph |
+----+-------------+--------+---------+
|  1 | Porsche     | Carrera|    NULL |
|  2 | Ferrari     | Dino   |    NULL |
|  3 | Lamborghini | Diablo |    NULL |
+----+-------------+--------+---------+
3 rows in set (0.00 sec)

mysql> _
```

Data can now be entered into the new column using the SQL **update** command, demonstrated on the next page.

Updating records

All data values in an existing table column can be changed using the SQL **update** command with the SQL **set** keyword, like this:

update *tablename* **set** *fieldname* = *newvalue* ;

More usefully, individual column values can be changed by adding a qualifier to the above syntax with the SQL **where** keyword so that only those values where the qualification is met will be changed. Typically the **where** qualifier will refer to the row's **id** number thereby selecting a particular cell in the specified column and row.

update *tablename* **set** *fieldname* = *newvalue* **where** *id* = *number* ;

This can be used in the 'cars' table example from the previous page to update the 'model' and 'top_mph' columns, as shown below:

Notice that the second update made in this example uses the value of the make column as its qualifier.

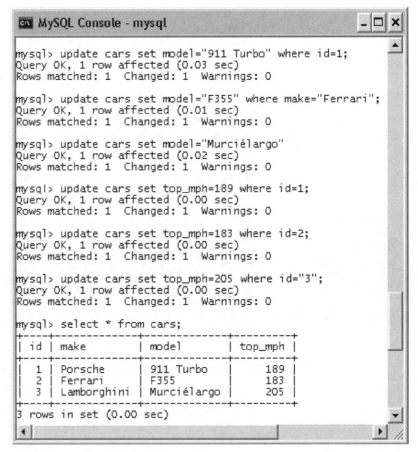

```
MySQL Console - mysql                                    _ □ X

mysql> update cars set model="911 Turbo" where id=1;
Query OK, 1 row affected (0.03 sec)
Rows matched: 1  Changed: 1  Warnings: 0

mysql> update cars set model="F355" where make="Ferrari";
Query OK, 1 row affected (0.01 sec)
Rows matched: 1  Changed: 1  Warnings: 0

mysql> update cars set model="Murciélargo"
Query OK, 1 row affected (0.02 sec)
Rows matched: 1  Changed: 1  Warnings: 0

mysql> update cars set top_mph=189 where id=1;
Query OK, 1 row affected (0.00 sec)
Rows matched: 1  Changed: 1  Warnings: 0

mysql> update cars set top_mph=183 where id=2;
Query OK, 1 row affected (0.00 sec)
Rows matched: 1  Changed: 1  Warnings: 0

mysql> update cars set top_mph=205 where id="3";
Query OK, 1 row affected (0.00 sec)
Rows matched: 1  Changed: 1  Warnings: 0

mysql> select * from cars;
+----+-------------+-------------+---------+
| id | make        | model       | top_mph |
+----+-------------+-------------+---------+
|  1 | Porsche     | 911 Turbo   |     189 |
|  2 | Ferrari     | F355        |     183 |
|  3 | Lamborghini | Murciélargo |     205 |
+----+-------------+-------------+---------+
3 rows in set (0.00 sec)
```

Deleting data, tables & databases

Records can be deleted from a table with the SQL **delete from** command followed by the table name. This needs to be used with some caution as the command **delete from** cars; would remove all the records from the 'cars' table instantly.

Specific records can be deleted from a table by adding a **where** qualifier to the **delete from** command in order to identify a row. For instance, the command to delete the third record in the 'cars' table would be:

delete from cars **where** id=3;

Specific columns can be deleted from a table using the SQL **alter table** command followed by the table name, then the **drop** keyword followed by the column name. For instance, the command to delete the 'top_mph' column from the 'cars' table would be:

alter table cars **drop** top_mph;

A complete table can be deleted from a database using the SQL **drop table** command followed by the table name. So the command to delete the 'cars' table would be:

drop table cars;

It is always a good idea to 'show tables' to check the contents before using 'drop database'.

An entire database can be deleted with the SQL **drop database** command followed by the database name. The 'garage' database that contained the 'cars' table can be deleted with the command:

drop database garage;

This deletes the database and also destroys any tables contained within it so must obviously be used with care.

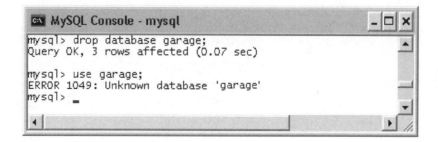

SQL queries

The basic SQL commands demonstrated in this chapter enable database tables to be created and filled with data. More advanced features of SQL allow the data to be queried for specific information. For instance, the 'cars' table at the bottom of page 156 could be searched, to find the details of any car with a top speed exceeding 200 mph, with this query:

select * **from** cars **where** top_mph < 200;

In this case there is just one record that fits the bill:

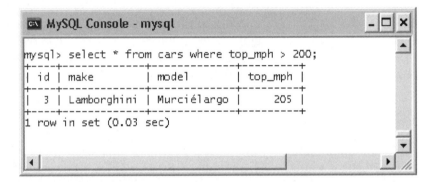

The ability to query data contained within databases is where the power of MySQL lies. More information illustrating the advanced features of the SQL language are given in the manual contained in the **Docs** folder of the MySQL installation directory.

Further details about SQL can also be found on the Internet in the MySQL Language Reference at www.mysql.com.

MySQL databases can be queried from JSP, using the exact same SQL command statements that are given in this chapter, thanks to Java DataBase Connectivity (JDBC).

Java contains a special class called **java.sql** for the purpose of accessing and processing data from a database.

Results of queries to a MySQL database can be returned to a special Java object called ResultSet that has several methods to retrieve the individual items of data. These can then be utilised by a scriptlet or included in the generated HTML response page.

Connecting JSP to MySQL

This chapter demonstrates how to establish a connection to MySQL databases from JSP using Java DataBase Connectivity (JDBC). It explains how to install a driver that acts as a connector between Java and MySQL. A sample MySQL database is created and a JSP log-in example demonstrates how to query its contents.

Covers

Chapter Thirteen

JDBC and MySQL

JDBC technology is an Application Programming Interface (API) that provides access to virtually any tabular data source from the Java programming language. It comprises a set of Java classes and interfaces which provide connectivity to a wide range of SQL databases, and other data sources such as spreadsheets.

Put simply, JDBC makes it possible to do three things:

- establish a connection to a database

- send SQL statements

- process the results

Before Java can access MySQL databases it is necessary to install a driver to allow MySQL to interface with JDBC. The most popular driver for this purpose is called MM.MySQL and is available for download at `http://mmmysql.sourceforge.net`.

Follow the link on this site to the download page then download the latest version, even if it says you must unjar it first. The file will be named something like **mm.mysql-2.0.11-you-must-unjar-me.jar**.

A **.jar** file is a Java compressed file whose contents can be extracted with the Java jar tool. If the jar file was located in **C:** the command to extract all its contents would look like:

C:>jar xvf mm.mysql-2.0.11-you-must-unjar-me.jar

Alternatively just rename the jar file with a **.zip** file extension and extract its contents with any zip tool, such as WinZip.

Either of these methods will extract two folders named **META-INF** and something like **mm.mysql-2.0.11**. The all-important driver file is contained inside the **mm.mysql-2.0.11** folder and is named, in this case, **mm.mysql-2.0.11-bin.jar**.

To make the driver available for JavaServer Pages it should be copied into Tomcat's **lib** folder where Tomcat automatically looks for compressed jar files.

A password database

With the MySQL JDBC driver safely installed in Tomcat's **lib** directory a database can be created to test the connection from a JSP application.

The test database has a single table containing records listing user names and passwords that can be used by a JSP log-in routine. It also holds custom log-in messages for each user.

This example creates a database named **register**, then a table named **users** inside that database. The **users** table has columns called **name**, **password** and **message** into which are inserted records for users named **guest**, **mike** and **linda**.

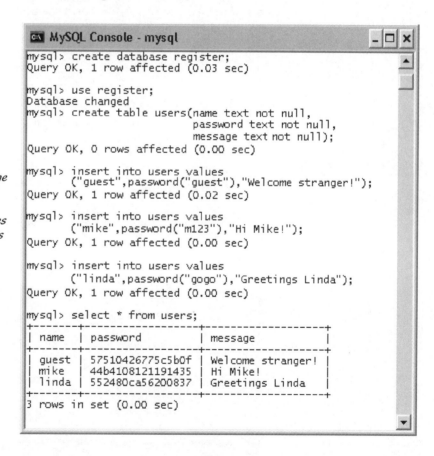

Notice how the MySQL password() function stores the passwords in encrypted form for security purposes.

The **users** table created above is used by the JSP examples given overleaf to test the connection to MySQL from JSP.

The password log-in page

In order to test the connection to the MySQL database containing the list of users and their passwords, created on the previous page, it is necessary to first present a page where the user can log-in.

The custom log-in message for approved users will be contained in a session attribute named **welcome**. This attribute is first sought by the code on this example page, named **db-login.jsp**, that will write out its value for logged-in returning users.

If the user has not already logged-in, a form is written on the page where the user can enter their name and password. On submission the form's details are processed by a second JSP page called **db-result.jsp**, as specified to the form's **action** attribute.

The user input will be passed to the processing page as parameters called **name** and **password**.

Do not rely on cookies – make URL rewriting a habit to avoid possible future problems with clients.

The example employs session tracking by URL rewriting with the **response.encodeURL()** function, described on page 108. This ensures that the log-in routine will work effectively on clients that do not, or cannot, accept cookies.

The log-in page is illustrated below and its complete source code is listed on the opposite page:

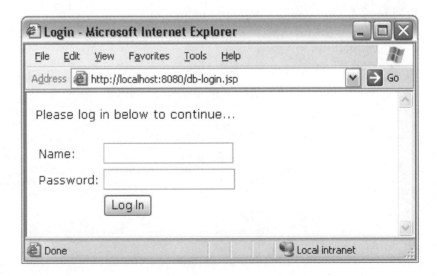

db-login.jsp

Specify an error page in the page directive for any error messages.

```jsp
<%@ page language="java"
        contentType="text/html"
        errorPage="errorpage.jsp" %>

<html>
  <head>
    <title>Login</title>
  </head>
<body>

<% if(session.getAttribute("welcome") != null) { %>

  <h3> <%= session.getAttribute("welcome") %> </h3>

<% } else { %>

  Please log in below to continue...
  <form method="post"
  action="<%= response.encodeURL("db-result.jsp")%> ">
  <table>
    <tr>
      <td>Name:</td>
      <td> <input type="text" name="name"> </td>
    </tr>
    <tr>
      <td>Password:</td>
      <td> <input type="password" name="password"> </td>
    </tr>
    <tr>
      <td></td>
      <td> <input type="submit" value="Log In"> </td>
    </tr>
  </table>
</form>

<% } %>

</body>
</html>
```

The user input from this form is processed by **db-result.jsp** page that is described and demonstrated on the next page.

Processing the password log-in

When a log-in attempt is submitted from the JSP page shown on the previous page it sends the user name and password entries as parameters to the **db-result.jsp** page for processing.

The entire source code of this page is shown opposite with comments added for greater clarity.

The processing page imports the **java.sql** class to make available its methods for making queries to the MySQL database called **register** that was set up on page 161.

Then it loads the driver from Tomcat's **ROOT/WEB-INF/lib** folder and establishes a connection to the database.

A statement is used to query the **users** table within the **register** database seeking a match for the name and password parameters contained in the page's request header.

When a record is found that matches both **name** and **password** columns the contents of that record's **message** column are returned to a RecordSet object for storage. This can then be assigned to a String variable for use by the scriptlet.

It is good practice to clean up the objects created in this routine using their **close()** methods when they are no longer needed.

When a match is made to the query this scriptlet assigns the **message** column value from the **users** table to a String variable called **message**, replacing its initial **null** value.

The hyperlink again employs URL rewriting to ensure that this log-in routine will work where cookies cannot be used.

The contents of the **message** variable are finally examined by the scriptlet which will assign them to a session attribute named **welcome** unless they are **null**. The result of the log-in attempt is displayed on the page together with a hyperlink to return the user back to the original log-in page, **db-login.jsp**.

A failed attempt will not set the **welcome** session attribute so that when the user returns to the original page the log-in form is displayed once more.

A successful attempt, on the other hand, does indeed set the **welcome** session attribute so that when the user returns to the original page it displays their custom welcome message.

...cont'd

db-result.jsp

The steps numbered 1–6 in this example can usefully be memorised as they are similar in every JSP database query.

Each stage of both failed and successful log-in attempts is depicted on the following pages.

```jsp
<%@ page language="java" contentType="text/html"
errorPage="errorpage.jsp" import="java.sql.*" %>

<html> <head> <title>Login</title> </head>
<body>

<%
  // 1. load the MySQL JDBC driver
  Class.forName("org.gjt.mm.mysql.Driver");

  // 2. open a connection to the "register" database
  Connection Conn = DriverManager.getConnection
                    ("jdbc:mysql://localhost/register");

  // 3. create a statement object for sending SQL
queries
  Statement Stmt = Conn.createStatement();

  // 4. place query results in a ResultSet object
  ResultSet RS = Stmt.executeQuery
    ("SELECT message FROM users WHERE name=
    '" + request.getParameter("name") + "'
    AND password=
    PASSWORD('" +request.getParameter("password")+"')");

  // 5. assign ResultSet's column 1 to a String variable
  String message = null;
  while (RS.next()) { message = RS.getString(1); }

  // 6. Clean up all objects
  RS.close(); Stmt.close(); Conn.close();
%>

<% if(message != null){
      session.setAttribute("welcome", message); %>
  <h3>Your login has succeeded. Thank you.</h3>
<% } else { %>
  <h3>Your login has failed, please try again.</h3>
<% } %>

<a href="<%= response.encodeURL("db-login.jsp") %>">
          Continue...</a>
</body> </html>
```

A failed password log-in attempt

 This attempt features an unrecognised user plus an unrecognised password entry of 'bingo'.

A successful log-in attempt

This attempt features a recognised user with the correct password of 'gogo'.

Post method versus Get method

The log-in form featured throughout this chapter specifies in its **method** attribute that the **post** method should be used when that form is submitted by the user. This method ensures that the form data is sent to the server in the request header.

There is no limit to the amount of data that can be sent with the **post** method and the posted data cannot be seen in the browser's address field.

The **post** method should, therefore, always be used when submitting large amounts of data or when submitting sensitive information, such as passwords or credit card details.

The default method used to submit a form, if no method is specified to its method attribute, is the **get** method. This is also the method used by hyperlinks to send a request to the server.

A query string can be added manually to the target file of a hyperlink to send parameter values with the get method like "target.jsp?name=mike".

Form data submitted by the **get** method is sent in a different manner to that used by the **post** method. It is first encoded to replace spaces and special characters then formed into a query string that begins with a **?** question mark. This is followed by the data as **name=value** pairs separated by **&** ampersands. Finally the entire query string is appended to the file name to be sent to the server as a parameter.

Some Web servers limit the amount of data that can be sent by the **get** method to 255 characters, making this method unsuitable for submitting large amounts of data.

The query string data can be seen in the address field of the browser making the **get** method unsuitable for submitting sensitive data. For instance, changing the form on page 165 to submit its data with the **get** method reveals the password, upon submission, in the address field after the sessionID like this:

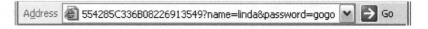

Generally use the **get** method for simple requests and the **post** method when some kind of processing is required on the server, such as updating a database or processing a purchase order.

A JSP online shop

This chapter is devoted to an example that demonstrates how JavaServer Pages can be used with a MySQL database to perform and record online transactions. JSP is the popular choice of many major UK retailers to provide shopping basket facilities for their ecommerce applications. Full example code is given to illustrate the flow of transactions.

Covers

Chapter Fourteen

Online shop overview

The first stage of building an online shop requires that consideration should be given to how the shopping process will progress. The shopper will browse through products on offer, selecting some for purchase as they go, then finally make payment for their selected items.

This process is identical to that of supermarket shopping where the shopper browses through products on the shelves, adding selected items to their shopping basket as they go, then finally makes payment at the checkout for their selected items.

Additional functions and validation could be added to the example code.

The shopping basket routine is familiar and is widely used throughout ecommerce applications. It will also be employed by the demonstration example in this book. The transaction flow through the example is illustrated below together with the names of the JSP page that will handle each stage:

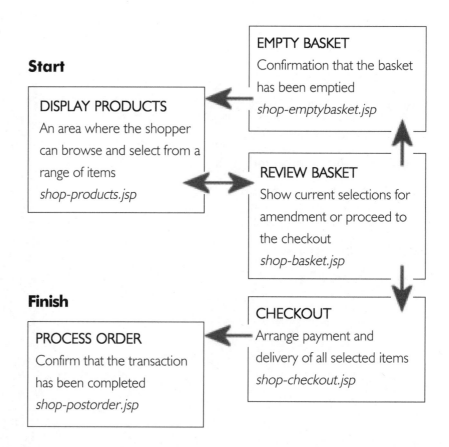

Start

DISPLAY PRODUCTS
An area where the shopper can browse and select from a range of items
shop-products.jsp

EMPTY BASKET
Confirmation that the basket has been emptied
shop-emptybasket.jsp

REVIEW BASKET
Show current selections for amendment or proceed to the checkout
shop-basket.jsp

CHECKOUT
Arrange payment and delivery of all selected items
shop-checkout.jsp

Finish

PROCESS ORDER
Confirm that the transaction has been completed
shop-postorder.jsp

Creating the shop database

The MySQL database that will be used in this example is called **shop** and contains three tables to store information.

The first table is called **items** and contains details about each product that will be offered for sale to the shopper – in this case the items are more books in the 'in easy steps' series. Each book is given a unique reference in the first column, called **item_id,** and other columns describe that book.

The **items** table will be accessed from JSP to populate a table listing the products on offer.

```
□...冒 shop
  └─□ items
  └─□ order_info
  └─□ orders
```

shop / items:

item_id	title	author	description	price
1	Java 2 in easy steps	Mike McGrath	Start Java programming	9.99
2	XML in easy steps	Mike McGrath	Using eXtensible markup	9.99
3	HTML4 in easy steps	Mike McGrath	Web pages with Style Sheets	9.99
4	CGI and Perl in easy steps	Mike McGrath	Server-side scripting simplified	9.99
5	JavaScript in easy steps	Mike McGrath	Dynamic interactive web pages	9.99
6	WAP in easy steps	Mike McGrath	Wireless markup for cellphones	9.99

shop / orders:

order_id	firstname	surname	address	city	postcode	card_number	card_type	totalvalue

shop / order_info:

orderinfo_id	order_id	item_id	quantity

Two other tables will be used to store information about the shopper's purchases when they submit an order.

A unique order number will be allocated when the shopper places their order. Each order number will be recorded in the **order_id** column of a table called **orders**. This table will also stores details about that shopper's name, address and credit card.

The third table, named **order_info**, creates a record for each item purchased that links the shopper's unique **order_id** number with the product's unique **item_id** number and the quantity required. A single order, with just one **order_id** number, can therefore, generate many **orderinfo_id** records where several different items are purchased.

Coding the shop's Java classes

The online shop example will use two custom Java classes to progress the shopper's selections through the transaction.

The first of these is the **Product** class listed below that provides an object model for the items to be offered for sale. It has variables that store details of id, title, price and quantity and has methods to return those values. In addition, another method returns the total price when multiples of that item are required.

Product.java / class

```java
public class Product
{
  /* define variables */
  String id, title;  int quantity; double price;

  /* define class
  public Product(String id, String title, double price)
  {
    this.quantity = 1;
    this.id = id;
    this.title = title;
    this.price = price;
  }

  /* define accessor methods */
  public String getId()    { return id; }
  public double getPrice(){ return price; }
  public int getQuantity(){ return quantity; }
  public String getTitle(){ return title; }
  public double getTotal()
  { return price * (double)quantity; }
}
```

Tomcat
- jakarta-tomcat-4.0.1
  - bin
  - classes
  - common
  - conf
  - lib
  - logs
  - server
  - webapps
  - work

The second class is named **ShoppingBasket** and is listed in full on the opposite page. This stores information about the items selected by the shopper inside a Vector object.

The **ShoppingBasket** class has methods to add and delete items from the basket and to calculate the total cost. Other methods return details of each item ordered and the quantity.

Both of these **.java** files are compiled into **.class** files which are placed in Tomcat's **classes** folder, ready to be used.

ShoppingBasket.java / class

Remember to import the java.util.* class package for Vector and Enumeration support.

See page 57 for more about using the Vector class.

```java
import java.util.*;
public class ShoppingBasket
{
  Vector products;
  public ShoppingBasket(){ products = new Vector(); }
  public void addProduct(Product product)
  {
    boolean flag = false;
    for(Enumeration enum=getProducts();
                          enum.hasMoreElements();)
    {  Product item = (Product)enum.nextElement();
      if(item.getId().equals(product.id))
        { flag=true; item.quantity++; break; }
    }
    if(!flag){ products.addElement(product); }
  }
  public void deleteProduct(String str)
  {
    for(Enumeration enum=getProducts();
                          enum.hasMoreElements();)
    { Product item = (Product)enum.nextElement();
      if(item.getId().equals(str))
        { products.removeElement(item); break; }
    }
  }
  public void emptyBasket(){ products = new Vector(); }
  public int getProductNumber(){ return products.size();
}
  public Enumeration getProducts(){
                        return products.elements(); }
  public double getTotal()
  {
    Enumeration enum = getProducts();
    double total; Product item;
    for(total=0.0D; enum.hasMoreElements();
                          total+= item.getTotal())
    { item = (Product)enum.nextElement(); }
  return total;
  }
}
```

Displaying the shop's products

The opening page of the online shop example makes a connection to the MySQL **shop** database and generates a HTML table containing all the records in the **items** table. A row counter alternates the background colour of each row.

Each row also contains a graphical button that includes the **item_id**, **title** and **price** of the item on that line as a query string linking back to this page. These are added to the variables of a **ShoppingBasket** JavaBean instance, named **basket**, so they can be accessed throughout the transaction.

Multiple items can be added to the shopping basket then its contents viewed by clicking the **View Basket** graphical hyperlink to the JSP page called **shop-basket.jsp**.

shop-products.jsp

```
<%@ page language="java" contentType="text/html"
        import="ShoppingBasket,Product"
        errorPage="errorpage.jsp" %>
<html>
<head> <title>Welcome to the Shop</title></head> <body>
<table width="385" border="0" cellspacing="0" >
<tr> <td colspan="4">More books from Mike McGrath:</td>
</tr> <tr>
 <td  colspan="4" align="right">

// hyperlink to view basket
<a href="<%= response.encodeURL("shop-basket.jsp") %>">
 <img src="images\viewbasket.gif"></a> </td>
</tr> <tr>
 <td><b>Ref</b></td> <td><b>Title</b></td>
 <td><b>Price</b></td> <td></td> </tr>

// get records from the items table in the shop database
<% Class.forName("org.gjt.mm.mysql.Driver");
   java.sql.Connection connection =
   java.sql.DriverManager.getConnection
                     ("jdbc:mysql://localhost/shop");
   java.sql.Statement stmt =
connection.createStatement();
   java.sql.ResultSet RS =
           stmt.executeQuery("SELECT * FROM items");
```

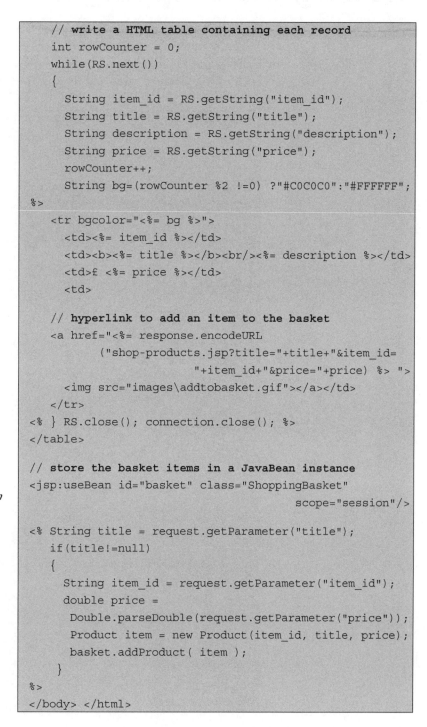

```
    // write a HTML table containing each record
    int rowCounter = 0;
    while(RS.next())
    {
      String item_id = RS.getString("item_id");
      String title = RS.getString("title");
      String description = RS.getString("description");
      String price = RS.getString("price");
      rowCounter++;
      String bg=(rowCounter %2 !=0) ?"#C0C0C0":"#FFFFFF";
%>

  <tr bgcolor="<%= bg %>">
    <td><%= item_id %></td>
    <td><b><%= title %></b><br/><%= description %></td>
    <td>£ <%= price %></td>
    <td>

    // hyperlink to add an item to the basket
    <a href="<%= response.encodeURL
            ("shop-products.jsp?title="+title+"&item_id=
                     "+item_id+"&price="+price) %> ">
    <img src="images\addtobasket.gif"></a></td>
  </tr>
<% } RS.close(); connection.close(); %>
</table>

// store the basket items in a JavaBean instance
<jsp:useBean id="basket" class="ShoppingBasket"
                                    scope="session"/>

<% String title = request.getParameter("title");
   if(title!=null)
   {
     String item_id = request.getParameter("item_id");
     double price =
     Double.parseDouble(request.getParameter("price"));
     Product item = new Product(item_id, title, price);
     basket.addProduct( item );
   }
%>
</body> </html>
```

The output generated by this JSP page can be seen on page 184.

Viewing the shopping basket

The **shop-basket.jsp** page writes a HTML table displaying the basket contents or a message if the basket is empty. Rows can be deleted and the basket can be emptied. Graphical hyperlinks point back to the products page and forward to the checkout.

shop-basket.jsp

```
<%@ page language="java" contentType="text/html"
        import="ShoppingBasket,Product,java.util.*"
        errorPage="errorpage.jsp" %>
<html>
<head><title>Your Shopping Basket</title></head> <body>
<jsp:useBean id="basket" class="ShoppingBasket"
                                    scope="session"/>
// delete items from the basket or write contents
<% String name = request.getParameter("name");
   if(name!=null)
   {
     if(name.equals("delete"))
     {
       String item_id = request.getParameter("item_id");
       basket.deleteProduct(item_id);
     }
   }
   if (basket.getProductNumber()!=0) {
%>
<table width="385" border="0" cellspacing="0" >
<tr>
 <td colspan="6">Items in your Shopping Basket:<br></td>
</tr>
<tr> <td>Ref</td> <td>Title</td> <td>Qty</td>
     <td>Price</td> <td>Total</td> <td> </td> </tr>

// write a HTML table row from bean contents
<% int rowCounter = 0;
   Enumeration products = basket.getProducts();
   while(products.hasMoreElements())
   {
     Product product = (Product)products.nextElement();
     rowCounter++;
     String bg=(rowCounter %2 !=0)? "#C0C0C0":"#FFFFFF";
%>
```

```
<tr bgcolor="<%= bg %>">
<td><%=product.getId()%></td>
<td><%=product.getTitle()%></td>
<td><%=product.getQuantity()%></td>
<td><%=product.getPrice()%></td>
<td><%=product.getTotal()%></td>
<td> <a href= "<%= response.encodeURL("shop-
    basket.jsp?name=delete&item_id="+product.getId()) %>
    ">Delete</a> </td>
</tr>
<% } %>
<tr> <td></td><td></td><td></td>
 <td><b>Total</b></td><td><%=basket.getTotal()%></td></
tr>
</table>    <br/><br/>

<a href="<%=response.encodeURL("shop-products.jsp")%> ">
<img src="images\toshop.gif" border="0"></a>
<a href="<%=response.encodeURL("shop-
                            emptybasket.jsp")%>">
<img src="images\emptybasket.gif" border="0"></a>
<a href="<%=response.encodeURL("shop-checkout.jsp")%> ">
<img src="images\tocheckout.gif" border="0"></a>
<% }else{out.print("Your Shopping Basket is Empty!"); %>
<br/><br/>
<a href="<%=response.encodeURL("shop-products.jsp")%> ">
<img src="images\toshop.gif" border="0"></a>
<% } %>   </body> </html>
```

If the basket is empty only a single hyperlink will be written.

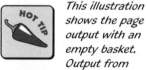

This illustration shows the page output with an empty basket. Output from this JSP page for a non-empty basket can be seen at the bottom of page 184.

At the shop checkout

In the **shop** example, the **shop-checkout.jsp** page, shown below, again lists all items in the shopping basket in exactly the same way used in the **shop-basket.jsp** page. The contents are displayed in a HTML table but the previous final column, offering to delete each row, is now omitted.

Additionally the page contains a HTML form with input fields where the shopper can enter their personal details. The form's action attribute assigns the **shop-postorder.jsp** page to process the form when the user pushes its submit button.

shop-checkout.jsp

Add verification to this page code to ensure that the form entries are complete and valid.

```
<%@ page language="java" contentType="text/html"
        import="ShoppingBasket,Product,java.util.*"
        errorPage="errorpage.jsp" %>
<html> <head> <title>Checkout</title> </head> <body>
<jsp:useBean id="basket" class="ShoppingBasket"
                                    scope="session"/>
<% if (basket.getProductNumber()!=0) { %>
<table width="385" border="0" cellspacing="0">
 <tr> <td colspan="5">Your order:<br><br></td> </tr>
 <tr> <td><b>Ref</b></td> <td><b>Title</b></td>
     <td><b>Quantity</b></td> <td><b>Price</b></td>
     <td><b>Total</b></td> </tr>
<%
   int rowCounter = 0;
   Enumeration products = basket.getProducts();
   while(products.hasMoreElements()) {
     Product product = (Product)products.nextElement();
     rowCounter++;
     String bg=(rowCounter %2 !=0)? "#C0C0C0" :
"#FFFFFF";
 %>
 <tr bgcolor="<%= bg %>"> <td><%=product.getId()%></td>
  <td><%=product.getTitle()%></td>
  <td><%=product.getQuantity()%></td>
  <td><%=product.getPrice()%></td>
  <td><%=product.getTotal()%></td> </tr>
 <% } %>
 <tr> <td></td><td></td><td></td> <td><b>Total</b></td>
     <td><%=basket.getTotal()%></td> </tr> </table>
```

shop-checkout.jsp (continued)

Notice that all hyperlinks in the shop example employ URL rewriting to ensure this routine will run when cookies are not available.

*Notice that the form inputs attribute names match the columns in the MySQL **orders** table, shown on page 171. An additional hidden input is used to send the order total to the table.*

```html
<b>Please Enter Your Details: </b>

<form method="post"
action="<%=response.encodeURL("shop-postorder.jsp")%> ">

<table width="385" border="1" cellspacing="0" >
<tr>        <td><b>First Name:</b></td>
  <td><input type="text" name="firstname" size=40></td>
</tr> <tr> <td><b>Surname:</b></td>
  <td><input type="text" name="surname" size=40></td>
</tr> <tr> <td><b>Address:</b></td>
  <td><input type="text" name="address" size=40></td>
</tr> <tr> <td><b>City:</b></td>
  <td><input type="text" name="city" size=40></td>
</tr> <tr> <td><b>Postcode:</b></td>
  <td><input type="text" name="postcode" size=10></td>
</tr> <tr> <td><b>Credit Card Type:</b></td>
  <td>
  <input type="radio" name="card_type" value="visa">
Visa
  <input type="radio" name="card_type"
value="mastercard"> Mastercard
  <input type="radio" name="card_type" value="amex">
Amex
  </td>
</tr> <tr> <td><b>Credit Card Number:</b></td>
  <td><input type="text" name="card_number" size=40></td>
</tr> </table>

<input type="hidden" name="totalvalue"
       value="<%= basket.getTotal() %> "> <br>

<a href="<%=response.encodeURL("shop-products.jsp")%> ">
<img src="images\toshop.gif" border="0"> </a>

<input type="submit" name="checkout"
       value="Press to Send Your Order">
</form>

<% } else { out.print("There are no items in your
                                shopping basket!");
  }%>  </body> </html>
```

Emptying the shopping basket

A shopper may elect to remove all current selections by pushing the 'Empty Basket' button on the **shop-viewbasket.jsp** page. In that case they are taken to the **shop-emptybasket.jsp** page that is listed below. This is a very simple page that merely calls the bean's **emptyBasket()** method to remove the basket items.

The page displays a message confirming that the basket is now empty and offers a link back to the main **shop-products.jsp** page so the user may choose new selections for the basket.

shop-emptybasket.jsp

All hyperlinks in the shop example employ URL rewriting so that the shopping basket will work when cookies are not enabled on the browser.

```
<%@ page language="java" contentType="text/html"
         import="ShoppingBasket,Product" %>

<html> <head> <title>Empty Basket</title> </head>
<body> <h3>Empty Shopping Basket:</h3>

<jsp:useBean id="basket" class="ShoppingBasket"
                                 scope="session"/>
<% basket.emptyBasket(); %>

Your shopping basket has been emptied. <br><br>

<a href="<%=response.encodeURL("shop-products.jsp")%> ">
<img src="images\toshop.gif" border="0"> </a>

</body> </html>
```

Processing the shopper's order

The purchase order in the **shop** example is finally processed by **shop-postorder.jsp** when the user submits the form on the **shop-checkout.jsp** page. This will connect to the MySQL **shop** database on the server and store all the submitted form values in the **orders** and **order_info** tables.

The database connection is made in the usual way using Java DataBase Connectivity and methods of the **java.sql** class. The connection process is identical to that used in the example in the previous chapter and detailed on page 165.

The first column of each shop table will automatically be set as these columns were created with an auto_increment modifier.

To add records to the database tables requires a special Java **PreparedStatement** object to pass all the form's attribute values to the database. In the **shop** example this object is called **Stmt** and is created with an SQL query describing the column pattern of the MySQL **orders** table.

The **setString()** method of the **Stmt** object is used to insert each form attribute value, in turn, into the defined pattern then these are applied to the table columns using the object's **executeUpdate()** method.

A unique order number can be assigned to each purchase order using a **getLastInsertID()** method that returns an index number of the last entry made into that table. In this example the index number is assigned to a variable named **order_id**.

The complete source code for shop-postorder.jsp is listed overleaf.

All individual **product_id** reference numbers and the **quantity** required are assigned to an Enumeration object called **products**. A loop through this object adds a record for each item ordered to the MySQL **order_info** table. This includes the unique order number stored in the **order_id** variable so that records in the **order_info** table can be cross-referenced with those in the orders table.

The **Stmt** and **connection** objects are closed when they are of no further use and the shopper's current selections are cleared by calling the bean's **emptyBasket()** method.

As a confirmation to the shopper the page displays an affirmation message and provides them with the unique **order_id** that has been allocated to their order.

The processing page source code

shop-postorder.jsp

```jsp
<%@ page language="java"  contentType="text/html"
         import="ShoppingBasket,Product,java.util.*"
         errorPage="errorpage.jsp"%>

<jsp:useBean id="basket" class="ShoppingBasket"
                                     scope="session"/>
<html> <head><title>Your Order Has Been Received</title>
</head> <body>

<%

    // 1. load the MySQL JDBC driver
    Class.forName("org.gjt.mm.mysql.Driver");

    // 2. open a connection to the "shop" database
    java.sql.Connection connection =
    java.sql.DriverManager.getConnection
                    ("jdbc:mysql://localhost/shop");

    // 3. assign SQL query and column pattern to variable
    String query =
        "INSERT INTO orders VALUES ('',?,?,?,?,?,?,?,?)";

    // 4. create a Statement object to send SQL queries
    java.sql.PreparedStatement Stmt =
                    connection.prepareStatement(query);

    // 5. get all form attribute values from the request
    // header and insert them into the Statement object
    // in the defined pattern...

    Stmt.setString(1,request.getParameter("firstname"));
    Stmt.setString(2,request.getParameter("surname"));
    Stmt.setString(3,request.getParameter("address"));
    Stmt.setString(4,request.getParameter("city"));
    Stmt.setString(5,request.getParameter("postcode"));
    Stmt.setString(6,request.getParameter("card_number"));
    Stmt.setString(7,request.getParameter("card_type"));
    Stmt.setString(8,request.getParameter("totalvalue"));

    // 6. add the record to the MySQL "orders" table
    Stmt.executeUpdate();
```

The query and info_query variables are only used to clarify the code – the SQL statements can be passed directly as the argument in the calls to the prepareStatement() method.

In real-world use, this data would be sent via a secure connection.

shop-postorder.jsp (continued)

```jsp
// 7. get an order number incremented from last order
long order_id =
((org.gjt.mm.mysql.PreparedStatement)Stmt).getLastInsertID();

    // 8. assign SQL query and column pattern to variable
    String order_info_query =
                "INSERT INTO order_info VALUES ('',?,?,?)";

    // 9. retrieve a list of basket contents from bean
    Enumeration products = basket.getProducts();

    // 10. add a record for each different selected item
    // to the MySQL "order_info" table...
    while(products.hasMoreElements())
    {
    Product product = (Product)products.nextElement();
    Stmt = connection.prepareStatement(order_info_query
);

    Stmt.setLong(1,order_id);
    Stmt.setInt(2,Integer.parseInt(product.getId()));
    Stmt.setInt(3,product.getQuantity());
    Stmt.executeUpdate();
    }

    // 11. clean up the objects
    Stmt.close();
    connection.close();

    // 12. empty the shopping basket
    basket.emptyBasket();
%>

Thanks for your order.
It will be processed within 24 hours.<br/>
Please note that your Order Number is No:
<%= order_id %> <br/><br/>

<a href="
  <%= response.encodeURL("shop-products.jsp") %> ">
  <img src="images\toshop.gif" border="0"> </a>

</body> </html>
```

Multiple order quantities are added to the quantity column of that record – an order for 3 of the same item adds a single record with a quantity value of 3, whereas an order for 3 different items adds 3 records each having a quantity value of 1.

This is the final page in the shopping basket routine. Turn to the next page to see how the whole thing looks in action.

Filling the shopping basket

Sample shopper, Joe Bloggs, clicks the button on row one twice to add two Java books to his basket then he clicks the button on row two to add one XML book to his basket. He proceeds to view his selections by clicking on the View Basket hyperlink.

Happy with his selections, Joe continues on to the checkout by clicking on the Proceed to Checkout button.

At the checkout, Joe enters his personal details for delivery and payment then he submits his order to the server for processing. The response confirms receipt of this order and Joe makes a note of his personal order number.

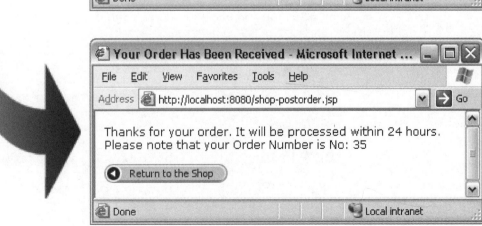

Receiving orders

Following submission of the sample order on the previous page a glance at the **shop** database confirms that the order details have been added in the **orders** and **order_info** tables as below:

A further Web application could be developed to process the received order details.

shop / orders:

order_id	firstname	surname	address	city	postcode	card_number	card_type	totalvalue
35	Joe	Bloggs	Anyplace	Any	AN7 0NE	123-456-7890	mastercard	29.97

shop / order_info:

orderinfo_id	order_id	item_id	quantity
60	35	1	2
61	35	2	1

This example, together with all the other examples given in this book will, hopefully, have given you a great introduction to JavaServer Pages so you can start creating JSP applications.

It is not feasible to include in a single book examples of every use to which JSP can be put as the possibilities are only limited by the developer's imagination. Many make extensive use of other features of the Java language such as the JavaMail API for email and the Java File class for reading and writing files.

A good starting point to discover more is Sun Microsystems' JSP website at `http://java.sun.com/products/jsp`.

Other useful websites featuring JSP samples, tutorials and resources are listed below and are well worth exploring for information and inspiration. Have fun developing with JSP!

Web Site	Address
JSP Resource Index	`http://www.jspin.com`
JSP Tags	`http://jsptags.com`
JSP Insider	`http://www.jspinsider.com`
jGuru (JSP faq)	`http://www.jguru.com`

Index

M

N

O

P

R

records   156
  updating   156
relational databases   148
removeElement() method   57
request object   64
  getCookies() method   118
  getHeader() method   64, 74
  getLocale() method   112
  getMethod() method   64
  getParameter() method   76
  getParameterValues() method   78
  getProtocol() method   64
  getRemoteAddr() method   64
  getRequestedSessionId() method   108
  getRequestURI() method   64
  getServerName() method   64
  getServerPort() method   64
request scope   97–98
response object   65
  addCookie() method   120
  addHeader() method   65
  encodeURL() method   108, 162
  getBufferSize() method   65
  getCharacterEncoding() method   65
  getLocale() method   65
  sendError() method   65
  sendRedirect() method   65
  setContentType() method   65
ResultSet object   158, 165
ROOT directory   19
rtexprvalue element   141

S

scope   97
  application   97
  attribute   32
  page   97
  request   97
  session   97
scripting elements   21, 26

security   11
server memory   110
session attribute   23
session data   122
session ID   104–105, 108
session object   67
  getAttribute() method   67, 122
  getCreationTime() method   108
  getId() method   67
  invalidate() method   67, 110
  setAttribute() method   67
session scope   97, 106
session tracking   108–109
setMaxAge() method   120
setName() method   32
setProperty action element   34–35, 127
setProperty wildcard   128–129
shopping basket   170, 184–185
short data type   49
SKIP_BODY constant   135, 144
spaces   47
SQL commands
  add   155
  alter table   155
  create database   150
  create table   151
  delete from   157
  drop   157
  drop database   157
  drop table   157
  insert into   154
  modify   155
  select * from   154
  set   156
  show databases   150
  show tables   151
  update   156
  values()   154
  where   156–157
SQL field modifiers
  auto_increment   153
  not null   153
  primary key()   153
  unique   153
SQL queries   158
stack trace   86
Statement   45
Statement object   165
statements - Java   51
static keyword   45
String data type   48
String object   62
  indexOf() method   74
  valueOf() method   62
String[] array variable   78

submitting form data   168
switch statements   56